Two Centuries

Two Centuries:
Caring for a Community

Principal Author
James M. Strosberg, MD, FACP, FACR

Editor
Louis S. Snitkoff, MD, FACP

Two Centuries: Caring for a Community

Copyright © 2010 Medical Society of the County of Schenectady, Inc

Cover design and photographic reproductions by Louis S. Snitkoff, MD

Printed in the United States of America

The Troy Book Makers • Troy, New York
www.thetroybookmakers.com

To order additional copies of this title,
contact your favorite local bookstore or visit www.tbmbooks.com

ISBN: 978-1-935534-662

Dedicated to the memory
of Ellis Kellert, MD

CONTENTS

SECTION 1

From Original Research

SECTION 2

From Individual Contributors

SECTION 3

Recent Past Presidents
June 2010 Membership and Elected Officers

PREFACE

"I do solemnly declare that I will honestly, virtuously & chastely conduct myself in the practice of Physic and Surgery with privilege of exercising which profession I am now to be invested, and that I will with fidelity and honor do everything in my power for the benefit of the sick committed to my care."

These are the words of the oath that was recited by all candidates for practice in the early days. They were found in the papers of Dr. Daniel Toll and published in the Centennial Celebration Booklet. Dr. Toll was a founder of the Medical Society of the County of Schenectady and served as its President from 1811 to 1824.

*   *   *

"...the laudable conservatism of the medical profession and slowness of people in all walks of life in accepting the new in any field of endeavor, especially by those over forty years of age..."

These are the words of Dr. Ellis Kellert, Ellis Hospital Pathologist and Past President of the Society, at the Annual Meeting in June 1959, on being honored for the 50th anniversary of his graduation from medical school.

FOREWORD

It has been a labor of love for me to participate in the creation of *Two Centuries: Caring for a Community* to help commemorate the bicentennial of our County Medical Society, which was founded in 1810.

Precedent had already been set for creating such a narrative and for observing milestones in the history of our organization. In 1908, anticipating the centennial celebration two years later, Dr. G. Marcellus Clowe proposed that a *"committee be appointed to write a history of our society... and prepare a celebration in some appropriate form."* Subsequently, the Society approved his motion to assess $7.50 per member to help defray the expense. The program for that evening is reproduced in this book.

For our sesquicentennial, the Society appropriated a total of $1000, charged $12 for the evening banquet, and made a profit of $400! This time, we approved Dr. Robert Kennedy's motion to assess each member $30 for the yearlong celebration.

However, our Society's interest in its roots has not been limited to 50-year cycles. As far back as 1891, there were efforts to *"collect pictures of past members and put them into albums...along with recollections of those who are still alive to remember them."* These fascinating historical sketches were published one hundred years ago in our centennial booklet, and some are included in this manuscript.

In 1935, for our quasquicentennial, the New York State (NYS) Journal of Medicine published an article by Dr. Ellis Kellert on the history of the Medical Society in Schenectady. More recently, in 1941 our members voted to authorize the sum of $60 to restore the formal portrait of Dr. Daniel Toll, our second president. Once again, in 1957, while located in the medical library at Ellis Hospital, he was found to need a brush up. At present, Dr. Toll's likeness is hanging in our Society office where he quietly observes our secretary, Helen Cover, perform her daily tasks, as he did her predecessor, Anita Smith, who retired in 2009 after 49 years of service.

In preparation for this project, I reviewed all existing minutes of the Society's meetings, along with countless letters and other documents. This was a bit time-consuming as there have been almost one thousand meetings! I hope that I have provided the reader with new information in an enjoyable format. Some subject areas were too complicated or extensive to review in depth. I chose to omit many of the controversial socioeconomic and political issues that were mentioned in the minutes; however, they could be included in a future study of public health policy.

Meeting minutes, by their nature, only provide a sketch, a cartoon or an outline of what actually transpired. They are not verbatim transcripts of the discussion that took place. And, the quality of the minutes varies from year to year, depending on the secretary. Often a very interesting matter is covered in great detail in the minutes, but it never re-appears in the minutes of future meetings. At times we only learn that a letter was received from "Dr. Doe," without any mention of its subject. Even when speakers are quoted, we cannot know the tenor of their voices.

Some things have remained the same over these 200 years, such as opposition to government regulation of health care. However, much has changed. For example, we now have physician advertising and hospital-employed physicians, both of which were considered to be unethical in the past.

The character of our Society has changed over the years. At one time, almost every physician in Schenectady was engaged in solo practice and most had offices on Union Street. (Of 108 physicians on the Medical Staff of City Hospital in 1959, 61 listed Union Street as their professional address.) Historically, most Schenectady physicians were members of the County Medical Society. Today, many physicians are members of large group practices, and a relatively small percentage are members. Only a minority of those attend our meetings regularly.

We were strictly a brotherhood until 1893 when Dr. Janet Murray joined as our first female member and we became a fellowship.

The Society functioned, in part, as a professional guild, addressing the economic concerns of its members. We had an active Sick Committee that visited all hospitalized and ailing members in their homes, often delivering fruit baskets. In 1870, our minutes note a donation of $15 to an indigent physician, and a contribution to help two destitute widows of members. And, in 1953 we voted an annual assessment to aid those in financial distress.

The late popular historian, Stephen Ambrose, said that if history is to be interesting it must be about people, because people are interesting. Our Society certainly has had its share of interesting people and I have interspersed biographical sketches of some of our more colorful forebears throughout the text. Four of our more prominent predecessors earned individual chapters.

In 1871, the Society called its first special meeting on the death of a member, and passed our first death resolution as a condolence to the physician's family. When Dr. A. Vedder died while out of town in 1878, the entire membership was notified by telegram. They donned black mourning badges and went en masse to meet his body at the train station. It is still our custom to make formal death resolutions and to attend the funerals of deceased members as a group to honor the memory of our colleagues.

Dr. Vedder, the most prominent surgeon of his time, was the first president of the reorganized Medical Society in 1870 and twice Mayor of Schenectady, as well as our delegate to the American Medical Association. He received his medical degree from the University of Pennsylvania and served a two-year internship, which was unusual for that time. He presented scientific papers at the State Medical Society meeting in 1875, including *"Diphtheria, Tracheostomy, and Recovery"* and *"Embolism of the Central Artery of the Retina."*

Dr Vedder established his reputation as a surgeon after only a few days in practice when, during a July 4th celebration at Crescent Park, two men lost their arms in the explosion of a muzzle-loading cannon. Dr. Vedder performed an amputation on one of the men, who recovered without incident. The second, less fortunate, man who had an identical injury was treated by another surgeon and fared less well. The operations were performed without anesthesia and the shrieks and groans of the poor men could be heard all over the city. Dr. Vedder's office was located on State Street, at the site of the former Daily Gazette building. As this was near the train tracks, he was often called upon to treat victims of railroad accidents.

Dr. Vedder, who also served as a Censor at Albany Medical College (AMC), was often consulted on difficult surgical and obstetrical patients, and was a pioneer in draining abscesses of the appendix. He was a tall man with a calm, dignified manner. He also maintained a flower garden, which attracted visitors from a wide area.

Currently, the officers of our Society are nominated by an elected nominating committee, and are elected by unanimous vote at the annual meeting. It was not always that way in the past, when offices were frequently contested. At the annual meeting in Jan 1895, Dr. Vedder (a different Dr. Vedder) and Dr. Kathan (the first of four generations of physicians) were both nominated for President, with Dr. Vedder winning by a vote of 9 to 6. Some elections had several candidates competing for the same office, and it took several ballots before one received a majority. (One can only wonder.)

In the past, meetings also served as social events. Members stayed long after the end of the program to fraternize and play cards. In the early days, when the membership was smaller, meetings were held at members' homes and a grand buffet was served. Several meetings took place at resorts on Saratoga Lake. The Alliance to the Medical Society (formerly known as the Auxiliary) held a boat ride on the Mohawk River in 1995. The weather was rainy and cold but everyone enjoyed listening to Doc Spring's Rehabilitated Dixieland Jazz Band. Other events included clambakes, coed volleyball games and dinner-dances.

Meeting minutes from years past must be interpreted in light of what was happening in Schenectady, our nation, and the scientific community at large during the period in which they were recorded. The history of our Society is intertwined with that of Schenectady, the medical staffs of all eight hospitals which existed at various times, the City and County Health Departments, the Schenectady County Chapter of Family Practice, the Medical Society of the State of New York (MSSNY), and the AMA.

Many of the socioeconomic and political actions taken by our Society were at the urging of these affiliated and parent institutions. A large section of the monthly Comitia Minora (our equivalent of a Board of Directors) minutes is taken up with communications from MSSNY and the AMA, as well as the NYS Department of Health (DOH) and various insurance companies. For many years, we were encouraged to oppose socialized medicine, not that encouragement was necessarily needed. Our Society's recent rejection of a resolution supporting single-payer national health insurance was an expression of grassroots, majority opinion.

Three of the most important functions occupying most of our two hundred years have faded in recent decades, each with good reason. The first was medical education. When you read the section on education you may be surprised by the quantity and quality of our past programs. However, with the advent of medical specialization and, somewhat later, the requirement for continuing medical education, the hospital clinical departments and specialty societies have taken over this responsibility.

A second function was public health. Schenectady physicians have been in the forefront of the fight against the infectious epidemics of the last two centuries. Some of this is not recorded in our minutes, as there are no records between 1841 and 1870, but we know from newspapers that are preserved on microfilm in the Schenectady County Public Library that there was a City and a County health officer. At times, there was disagreement within the medical profession concerning the science of disease or the best public health approach (e.g., the Schick Test for diphtheria), but the physicians were always committed to do what was best for their own patients and for the community at large, given the evidence available to them.

A third function, which has diminished but not disappeared, was concern for the livelihood of our members. Our Society was, and is, composed of colleagues and not competitors. For most of our history, physicians were also small businessmen engaged in solo private practice. In the past, our Society guarded against what it perceived to be unfair, outside competition. In the early years, this included practitioners of alternative methods, such as homeopathy. More recently, the Society, along with MSSNY and the AMA, has fought against burdensome laws and regulations and inadequate reimbursements for our services. Despite the economic realities of private practice, we have always remained mindful of our patients' best interests.

As we look back on our history, we must avoid the temptation to be judgmental about the actions of our predecessors. Existing records often do not provide us with enough information to put their decisions in proper societal context and time machines do not yet exist. Nevertheless, if we wish to take pride in the foresight of those who came before us, we must also feel some remorse for what, in retrospect, may seem to be poor judgment even though seemingly reasonable at the time.

In recent decades, the practice and the business of medicine have changed substantially. In spite of this, our Society has continued to be a catalyst for improvement of the public health and welfare. While many individual physicians, due to their practice circumstances, are less involved in day-to-day practice management, we continue to dedicate ourselves to serving our patients and our community.

In my opinion, our greatest contributions have occurred during the past 50 years with the help and support of the Alliance. Many of these are described in the chapters that follow.

*　　*　　*

The minutes of our meetings from 1870 through the present time are housed in the Society office and are in very good condition, except for poor penmanship; some things never change! They are the basis for most of our history, along with Hospital on the Hill by Larry Hart, old editions of Schenectady newspapers from the microfilm collections at the Schenectady County Library, records from the Schenectady County Historical Society and the Efner History Center in Schenectady City Hall. I have also referred to the Encyclopedia of Union College History, edited by Wayne Somers, meeting minutes of the Ellis Hospital Board of Trustees dating back to 1885, Ellis Hospital Annual Reports, manuscripts from Medical Society Historian Dr. Roy C. Keigher, and various Medical Society letters and records, including the centennial and ses-quicentennial booklets.

In most references to meetings, I have cited the month and the year for the benefit of read-ers who wish to obtain more information from the source documents. In mentioning specific names, I have tried to include those that would be meaningful to our present members. I made a particular effort to include relatives of current members. The Purcell, Jameson, Kathan and Clowe families have had 3 generations of members. Following precedent in the minutes, I have sometimes not included first names.

ACKNOWLEDGMENTS

I wish to thank my colleague, Dr. Louis Snitkoff, for serving as Editor of this book and my brother, Professor Martin Strosberg of Union Graduate College, for his technical assistance and encouragement. In addition, I am grateful for the assistance and support of the following individuals: Katherine Chansky, Librarian of the Schenectady County Historical Society; Ed Reilly and Frank Taormina, President and Past-President of the Historical Society; Chris Stater, Medical Librarian of Ellis Hospital; Cindy Seacord, Managing Archivist of the Efner Center; Donald Keefer, former Scotia-Glenville historian; Anita Smith and Helen Cover, secretaries of the Medical Society; and, especially, my wife Margo Strosberg for her technical advice.

I also wish to thank those who have contributed chapters describing what I believe have been our greatest accomplishments—those of the last 50 years, and some of our most distinguished members. They include: Dr. Nadarajah Balasubramaniam, Ms. Cristine Cioffi, Dr. John Fulco, Mrs. Marie Gorman, Mrs. Lois Gullott, Dr. Richard Gullott, Dr. Michael Jakubowski, Dr. Grace Jorgensen, Dr. Carolyn Jones-Assini, Dr. Richard Lange, Dr. Arnold Ritterband, Prof. Martin Strosberg, and Mrs. Rose Tischler.

James M. Strosberg, MD

2010

EDITOR'S NOTE

The fascinating history of the Medical Society of the County of Schenectady suggests that, over the past two centuries, health care has become woven into the fabric of our community. This may be common among municipalities of our size, where physicians live and work, make friends and forge professional relationships, help drive the local economy, serve as volunteers, educators and civic leaders, and labor tirelessly to ensure the health and improve the lives of their neighbors.

As a physician in this community for 30 years, I have been privileged to work beside many wise and talented colleagues. Collectively, they—and their predecessors—have endowed Schenectady with a depth and breadth of medical expertise that has long been envied by similar localities in Upstate New York. Many of the accomplishments chronicled in this volume demonstrate the compassion, dedication, resourcefulness and foresight of physicians who have served here. For them, health care has been a calling and not a commodity.

I wish to thank my collaborator and principal author, James Strosberg, MD, for his countless hours of research and for his substantial commitment of time and energy to this project. In addition, the material contributed by many others has enriched this text in ways that would not have been possible otherwise. Much like the care of a patient, production of this publication was a coordinated effort executed smoothly by a team of capable and concerned individuals.

On a final note, *Two Centuries* is not intended to be an exhaustive or academic account of our history. Perhaps that is an endeavor for another time. Nonetheless, we have taken reasonable steps to ensure the accuracy of the material presented herein and we regret any errors or omissions that may have occurred.

Louis S. Snitkoff, MD

August 2010

SECTION 1

From Original Research

By James M. Strosberg, MD
Principal Author

EARLY HISTORY

The Medical Society of the County of Schenectady was formed in 1810, pursuant to an act of the NYS Legislature in 1806 *"incorporating Medical Societies for the purpose of regulating the Practice of Physic and Surgery in the State."* Schenectady County separated from Albany County in 1809, and the following year ours became the thirty-sixth society in the state. In 1810, the population of our county was 10,000, half of whom lived in the City of Schenectady and in what now are the Towns of Rotterdam and Glenville. There were also about 300 African-American slaves. The State finally abolished slavery on July 4, 1827. (In 1799, our legislature passed the Gradual Manumission Act, phasing out slavery over a 28-year period.)

Our first meeting was held at the County Court house on June 10. Forty-one members signed the charter and elected officers. Their signatures are reproduced on page 13. The by-laws (page 14), which were adopted on the following day, required that meeting notices be published in at least two newspapers. Can you imagine a city of five thousand having two newspapers? Members were fined twelve-and-a-half cents for being *"absent after the President [had] assumed the Chair and the Secretary [had] called the roll."*

The first president was Dr. Archibald Adams, whose father and grandfather were also Schenectady physicians. His grandfather, Dr. William Adams, was born in Ireland and was a friend of Sir William Johnson, a commander in the French and Indian War. Adams settled in Schenectady in 1757 and practiced for 70 years. He served as a surgeon under Sir William at the Battle of Lake George. Consistent with his friendship with Johnson, he was a Tory during the American Revolution and was twice summoned before the Committee of Safety, once to be bailed, and was later banished behind enemy lines. He must have had a good reputation as a physician because, unlike many Tories, he remained in our new nation and did not flee to Canada.

Like many doctors of his time, grandfather William also ran a drug store and dry goods store with his son, Dr. James Adams, who died in 1801 at age 33. When William was 97, he traveled to Litchfield, Connecticut to visit his granddaughter. He died in 1827 at 99 years of age.

Serving as an officer of our Society back then must have been very demanding. Our first Treasurer, Dr. Cornelius Vrooman, died in 1811 at age 30, within a year of taking office. That year, in addition, our founding President, Dr. Archibald Adams, and founding Vice President, Dr. Anderson, also died. Dr. Anderson contracted yellow fever while returning from a trip to New Orleans, though the disease was still endemic in the Capital Region at that time. In 1813, the Schenectady Cabinet reported many cases and some deaths in Albany but only a few cases and no deaths in Schenectady. This fact was emphasized in newspaper reports by Union College to help recruit and retain boys from Southern states, many of whom came North for their education to escape diseases, such as malaria, that were endemic in the warm and swampy South.

The original purpose of the Society was to license physicians. This function was given to the Board of Censors. New York, as a British Colony, had been regulating medical practices since 1690. The mayor, a judge, and a lawyer in each town examined applicants; there was a physician-consultant available if needed. To be eligible for a NYS license in 1810, a candidate had to apprentice to a physician for four years; however, if he or she had attended one of the three medical schools in the United States at that time, only three years of apprenticeship were required. Around the time of the Revolution, this authority passed to a New York Supreme Court judge.

The minutes from 1810 are difficult, if not impossible, to read because of the handwriting (page 17). The original documents from 1810 thru 1841 have been kept at the Schenectady County Historical Society since 1948, and are available to the public for research. It is still thrilling to hold the yellowed paper with brown ink and realize that these documents were written only 3 months after Thomas Jefferson left the White House. The meetings were usually held quarterly and most of the agenda was consumed by the Board of Censors recommending candidates for licensing, and electing delegates to the State Society. The minutes contain almost no reference to the medical issues of the day. At the Historical Society, there are no minutes between 1812 and 1824, and none after 1841. At that time, Medical Society activity was suspended until 1870 for reasons that are largely lost to history.

Austin Yates, in his History of Schenectady County published in 1902, states *"no business of any importance was done in 1841...internal dissension had destroyed the efficiency of the society, as such, and it soon ceased to have an existence."* Unfortunately, he does not site his sources. It is not clear what

(Right) Subscribers to original bylaws: Thomas Dunlop, Daniel J. Toll, Alexander G. Fonda, Cornelius Vrooman, Robert Wolmsley, Abraham D'Lamter, John Wood, Daniel McDougall, P.B. Knoxon, J. Berkley, E. B. Sprague, I. W. Conklin, Stephen Remington, John B. Judson, Archibald H. Adams, Daniel Lowe, Joseph Koon, J. C. Macoffin, John S. Tonelier, Benjamin F. Joslin, Edward H. Wheeler, Abram W. Van Woert, Edgar Fonda, A. J. Prine, Andrew Truax, L. Sprague, James Chandler, Ora Squire, A. M. Vedder, Benjamin Weeks, John S. Crawford, N. Marselius, J. Stackpole, Edwin A. Young

Subscribers Names

Thos. Dunlap

Danl. J. Wolff

Abraham DLamatter

John Wood

Danl. McDougall

C. B. Sprague

J. Wilcocklin

Nathan Remington

Inq. B. Judson

Joseph Hoon

Benjn. F. Joslin

Edwd. H. Wheeler

Abram Van Noah

Andrew Smart

James Chandler

A. M. Vedder

Benjn. Weeks

John S. Crawford

Marselis

F. Stackpole

Edwin A. Young

Laws of the Medical Society of the
County of Schenectady —

Whereas by an act of the Legislature of the State of
New York, entitled an Act to incorporate Medical
Societies for the purposes of regulating the Practice
of Physic & Surgery in this State passed April 4th 1806
the Physicians & Surgeons of each County in the
State are authorized to form themselves into Societies
for the Purposes mentioned in the Act, & to make
such Bye laws & Regulations as they may think
necessary & proper, the same not being repugnant
to the Laws of the State or the Bye laws of the State
Medical Society. We the Physicians & Surgeons
the City & County of Schenectady having formed
ourselves into a Medical Society incorporated by
the aforesaid Act do adopt the following Bye laws.

Article 1st The officers of the Society shall consist of a
President, Vice President, Secretary, Treasurer, & not
less than three nor more than five Censors to be
chosen by ballot annually at the Anniversary
meeting of the Society.

Article 2d The President shall preside at all the meetings, preserve Order, put all Questions, declare the
decisions of the Society, & in case of an equal division
shall have the casting Vote; he shall also appoint
all committees, unless the Society choose to appoint
them by special Resolution; In the President's absence

Original bylaws

legal authority issued medical licenses during those decades, but Yates suggests that the Board of Censors continued to function for the purpose of licensing new doctors.

The Censors questioned the candidates on many subjects including "Anatomy, Physiology, Surgery, Midwifery, Materia Medica, Pharmacy, Theory and Practice of Physic, and Chemistry." There could not have been many questions about the last two subjects because little was known at the time. Presumably, the "theory and practice of Physic" dealt with more than enemas and cathartics! Union College had just opened its Department of Chemistry and Mineralogy in 1810. The Physics (not *physic*) Department—then known as Natural Philosophy—started five years earlier, and was equipped with scientific instruments from England to teach astronomy, mechanics, optics, electricity and magnetism. The College was founded in 1795.

In 1842, the authority to grant medical licenses was given to the State Supreme Court Judges, and was likely returned to the medical societies around 1870. As recently as 1876, new members were inducted who were "licensees" of Albany County or Schenectady County, and not graduates of a medical school. In 1880, the State Legislature abolished the right of county medical societies to grant medical licenses, transferring the authority to the Board of Regents. In the early 1900s, the authority was once again transferred to the Department of Health (DOH). In 1910, the Flexner Commission, sponsored by the Carnegie Foundation and the Council of Medical Education of the AMA, surveyed all 155 medical schools in the United States, many of which were only diploma mills. Some schools granted degrees to students who had never even examined a patient. More than half of them were forced to close or merge with other institutions. All candidates for medical school were now required to have completed at least 2 years of scientific study at the college level.

The Society reorganized itself in January 1870. Those who joined were known as "charter members." In addition to the regular officers, our Society eventually elected delegates to the Medical Societies of Albany, Montgomery and Fulton counties, as well as to the State Society, the Fourth District, and the AMA. In those pre-automobile days, charter members came from Mariaville, Scotia, Schenectady, Duanesburg, Pattersonville, Quaker Street, Sloansville, Esperance, and even the Saratoga County villages of Rexford Flats and West Charlton.

Why did Schenectady doctors feel a need to re-establish the Medical Society in 1870? The answer can easily be found in the initial minutes, which state... *"none but REGULAR physicians may be members of the society."* At that time, throughout NYS, there was competition between "regular" (allopathic) and "non-regular" or "irregular" physicians, of which there were several types. The largest number were homeopaths, who practiced in homeopathic hospitals in Buffalo, Rochester and Syracuse, and at two homeopathic medical schools in New York City (NYC).

The term allopath (i.e., we traditional physicians) was coined in the early 19th century by Dr. Samuel Hahnemann, the German founder of homeopathy, to distinguish us from them. "Allo" means "other," "homeo" means "the same," and "pathos" means "disease." The basic tenet of homeopathy was "like cures like." For example, a very tiny amount of coffee could cure insomnia. Traditional medicine was, and is, based upon the principle of treating with medications that have a different effect from the disease itself. Hahnemann's students brought homeopathy to America, where it flourished. In 1900, there were one thousand homeopathic hospitals in the United States and twenty-two homeopathic medical schools, the last of which closed around 1922.

We must keep in mind that, for many years, homeopathic physicians frequently had better patient outcomes than we did. In 1810, we only had two main treatments, phlebotomy and calomel, which was a cathartic. Often, we did more harm than good. However, a Schenectady newspaper suggested phlebotomy as a useful treatment for the cholera epidemic of 1824. Homeopathic treatments, in comparison, were unlikely to cause harm, they may have had a placebo effect, or the patient may have recovered despite treatment. In any event, the patient naturally gave credit to the homeopathic remedy.

In 1906, Dr. James Van Ingen (one of "us") would sometimes be called for a second opinion by the family of a patient then undergoing treatment by Dr. Swit, a homeopathic physician. Dr. Van Ingen, in an attempt to discredit homeopathy, would ask the family to give him all of the medicine prescribed by the homeopath and then drink it all on the spot. He would then face the patient and declare, "there you are, not a bit of potency in all that medicine." Dr. Swit got his revenge, however. He gave each of his patients an unlabeled bottle of ipecac with instructions to take only one drop each week. The next time Dr. Van Ingren swallowed all of his patient's "impotent" homeopathic medicine, he became violently ill.

We have no record of any meeting between Dr. Van Ingen, the allopath, and Dr. Swit, the homeopath, following the ipecac incident. Dr. Van Ingen was 6 feet 3 inches tall and weighed over 300 pounds. He was eccentric, with a bad temper and his numerous squabbles led to litigation and, also, to fist fights. He was a familiar figure around town, wearing a beard, cape and broad-brimmed hat, and he usually carried a whip or a gun on his person.

Dr. Van Ingen had a great fund of medical knowledge, some of which he acquired in Paris. He was a pioneer in orthopedics, one of the first to use counter-extension in the treatment of fractures, and his articles were quoted in textbooks. He was a member of St. George's Episcopal Church and always finished the entire portion of communion wine citing from Scripture, "Drink ye all of this." Dr. Van Ingen was a Union College graduate (Class of 1840) and was the commencement orator. He was a medical officer during the Civil War, serving with the 18th Infantry New York Volunteers.

Minutes of the Medical Society of the County of
Schenectady——

Schenectady June 11th, 1810

Agreeable to the Act incorporating Medical Societies for the purpose
of regulating the Practice of Physic & Surgery in this State, passed
April 4th, 1806, the Physicians & Surgeons of the County of
Schenectady convened at the Court Room & proceeded to the
Election of Officers necessary for their organization as prescribed by
Law. Doctr Richd H. Adams was elected President, Doctr Wm Ander-
son Vice President, Doctr Alexr J. Fonda Secretary & Doctr Corns
Vrooman Treasurer. Doctrs Thos Dunlap, Alexr J. Fonda &
Corns Vrooman were appointed a Committee to draft a
Code of Laws & report them to the Society for their Ratifica-
tion. Resolved That this Society meet annually the
2d Tuesday in June at 3 OClock P.M. in the Court Room
which time as prescribed by the above united Law shall
forever thereafter be the Anniversary meeting of this Society.
                                        Adjourned——

Schenectady June 12th, 1810

At the Anniversary Meeting of the Medical Society of the
County of Schenectady convened at the Court Room,
the Roll being called Doctr Richd H. Adams & Abm Delamater
absent. The Committee appointed to draft a Code of Bye Laws
made a Report of the same, which was acceded to & ratifi-
ed by the Society. Doctrs Corns Vrooman, Wm Anderson,
Thos Dunlap Daniel Toll & Abm Delamater were elected
Censors of this Society. In conformity to the privilege granted each County Medical Society Daniel McDougall
was unanimously chosen as a suitable Person to attend the Lectures in the City of New York on the different
Branches of Medicine.   Adjourned——

Meeting minutes of June 11 and 12, 1810

His father, Dr. Dirck Van Ingen, was born in Holland. He was a noted Revolutionary War surgeon and commanded the Continental Army Hospital located on Lafayette St. He was also a Founder of Union College, and maintained his office at 10 North Church Street.

Society minutes are replete with charges made by members against the practice of non-regular physicians or the unethical practices of regular physicians. In 1841, Dr. Sprague complained that Dr. Conklin, an original signer of our 1810 Bylaws, obtained his credentials fraudulently but nothing more is recorded with respect to this allegation. In 1876, the Ethics Committee discussed an advertisement by a doctor, certainly an uncommon practice of the day. At a meeting in 1883, the Society authorized the Board of Censors to "investigate all physicians practicing who are not qualified, including midwives, and report them to the district attorney for prosecution."

In January 1889, the Censors were asked to investigate a case of two members manufacturing and selling a patent medicine. This was a serious breach of ethics. In fact, at the annual meeting of 1812, an amendment to the by-laws passed unanimously, stipulating *"that no person being a member of the Society shall hold any nostrum or specific for the cure of a disease under the penalty of forfeiting his seat in the same."* The two members were notified to appear to defend themselves. Failure to do so would imply guilt and they would be expelled from the Society. One doctor appeared and promised that, in the future, he would not place his name on the bottle. The minutes do not indicate what became of the second doctor.

At the April 1898 meeting, the Censors were asked to investigate a case of peritonitis treated by an "Indian doctor" and, in September of that year, they were authorized to employ counsel to prosecute an eye specialist practicing when he had no right to do so. (Ophthalmology was one of the earliest specialties, partly due to the technological advance of the ophthalmoscope.) In June 1904, the Censors were empowered to obtain evidence and prosecute any druggist prescribing medication. At the April 1914 meeting, Dr. Samorini presented an advertisement of an Italian doctor practicing without a license and, in 1916, the Censors were authorized to employ a private detective to investigate irregular physicians.

In 1898, we received a notice from the State Society urging us to take action against a bill in the legislature permitting osteopathic physicians to practice and we received regular communications warning against associating with homeopaths and osteopaths. In January 1903, the Censors wrote the State Society to inquire if there had ever been any proceeding against osteopaths, and what the result had been. In October 1905, we wrote to our representatives in the State Senate and Assembly, alleging that osteopaths were *"detrimental to the public."* In September 1933, the Comitia Minora discussed the removal of tonsils by electro-coagulation by an osteopath, and referred the matter to the State.

Composite photograph of membership, 1894

W. T. Clute   J. A. Heatley   H. Z. Van Zandt   C. G. Briggs   C. F. Clowe   A. T. Veeder   Dr. Raymond
H. A. Kurth   Dr. Van Allen   D. L. Kathan   Chas. Hammer   Robt. Fuller   G. E. McDonald   W. Reaggles   Dr. Barry
Dr. Van Epps   H. V. Mynderse   W. L. Pearson   C. C. Duryee   Dr. Burland   Dr. Brownell   J. L. Schoolcraft
Maurice A. Perkins   Dr. McKay   Janet Murray   J. McEncroe   L. T. Vedder   M. G. Planck

In 1934, legislation finally passed that permitted osteopaths to practice and enabled their use of local anesthetics and anodyne. (An *anodyne* is defined as an analgesic, but it also has a more specific meaning as a therapeutic light.) State Senator Baxter voted for the bill, despite receiving many telegrams from members in opposition. However, thirty years later, the AMA still did not permit doctors of medicine to have a professional relationship with doctors of osteopathy.

Now, fast forward to October 1972, 38 years after osteopaths were granted the right to practice. Dr. Staunton, citing his "eye-opening" experience with AMC neurology residents with osteopathic backgrounds rotating on the Ellis Hospital neurology service, proposed that osteopaths be accepted into the County and State Society. Many spoke in favor of this resolution. At the December 1972 meeting, Dr. Steeper of the Hospital and Professional Relations Committee reported that there was divergence of opinion among the osteopaths on desirability of membership in our societies.

At the January 1973 meeting, our Society voted to send Dr. Staunton's resolution to the State Society and, at its Annual Convention in February 1974, the House of Delegates voted unanimously to allow osteopaths to join the State Society. This decision cleared the way for battle with the next adversary—chiropractic!

CONTAGIOUS DISEASES

For many years, the primary causes of death in Schenectady, as in the rest of America, were the contagious diseases. In 1855, 21% of all deaths in Schenectady were caused by tuberculosis, which was the number one killer during the last half of the 19th century. More about this dreaded disease can be found in the history of Glenridge Hospital. However, with subsequent advances in medical science, these infections could be prevented and treated. Thus, in 1988, 75% of the 1,533 Schenectadians who died lost their lives to heart disease, cancer and stroke.

Smallpox

The first public health challenge our new Medical Society faced was smallpox. The citizens of Schenectady must have been terrified of this disease. During the American Revolution, a Continental Army barracks housing a 400-bed hospital was located on Lafayette Street and, undoubtedly, many soldiers stationed there contracted smallpox and died. (Many years later, 57 bodies were exhumed from the site of the old hospital burial ground and moved to Vale Cemetery with full military honors.) Schenectady was on the primary military route to the West during the War of 1812; soldiers traveling between Army bases had already contracted smallpox, thereby presenting a public health risk to the residents of Schenectady. This disease had killed about 90 percent of the Native Americans in the Dutch New Netherlands (which included the Capital District) and would remain a serious threat for decades to come. In 1850, for example, 1,000 residents of NYC died of smallpox out of a population of 500,000.

Unfortunately, in 1775, doctors and others were ordered to desist from inoculating with material from the pustules of smallpox patients because some recipients did not develop immunity and died of the disease. According to documents in the Efner History Center at Schenectady City Hall, the prohibition against inoculation emanated from an organization called the Schenectady District Committee. Nonetheless, during the darkest days of the Revolution in 1777, General George Washington had his troops inoculated with smallpox virus derived in this fashion. This decision (against the advice of many physicians) probably saved his army—and our infant country.

In 1796, Dr. Edward Jenner of England was credited with giving the first smallpox vaccination consisting of cowpox, or vaccinia virus. (*Vacca* is the Latin word for cow.) His patients almost always survived the vaccine, in contrast to some of the recipients of smallpox-derived vaccines, who contracted the disease and died. Jenner subsequently challenged his patients with exposure to live smallpox and none of them became infected.

The early officers of our Medical Society showed confidence in the scientific method of Jenner's experiment. With great leadership and foresight, they placed this notice in the September 14, 1814 issue of the *Schenectady Cabinet:*

"We the subscribers, physicians of the City of Schenectady, do most cheerfully recommend Dr. Sylvanus Fansher as a competent person for vaccinating. As some of the citizens have expressed the desire of having a Kine Pock introduced, there being no doubt many who have not received it in this city, we respectfully solicit the attention of the citizens......as the season is favorable to its introduction. We have just been informed that the Small Pox has lately broke out in several places in the Army and amongst the citizens, one not far distant from this place." [Note: "Kine Pock" was an old Dutch term for cowpox]

In addition to the physicians, Union College President Eliphalet Nott signed the letter. Clinics were held over four days at the Dutch Church, at a private home on Green St. and at Gates Tavern on State Street. Patients were requested to report back to the clinics one week and two weeks post-vaccination for a checkup. The citizenry took up a collection to pay for vaccination of the destitute and Dr. Fansher called at their homes. Apparently, not everyone received the kine pox vaccination, because death notices appeared in the local newspapers listing the cause of death as "small pox." By 1977, smallpox was eradicated globally by the World Health Organization (WHO).

Cholera

At least 4 of the original signers of our 1810 bylaws played an active role in the Asiatic cholera pandemic of 1834. Cholera is a bacterial disease spread by fecal contamination of food or drinking water and causes severe diarrhea that can lead to fatal dehydration in a matter of hours. The *Schenectady Cabinet,* published at 10 Union Street, kept our city informed of the progress of this disease westward across Europe and across the Atlantic to Montreal and down the Hudson-Champlain Valley. (According to a June 9, 1834 letter, *"[there are] 400 foreign ships quarantined with 20,000 emigrants including one ship from Dublin with 42 dead."* The City of Troy quarantined 180 immigrants on Green Island in the Hudson River. Cholera arrived in Schenectady by way of the Erie Canal in early July. However, the Fourth of July celebration was not cancelled, even though there were 10 dead in Albany and one in Guilderland.

During this period, many troops passed westward through Schenectady by canal boat to fight the Black Hawk War, bringing cholera along with them. General Winfield Scott and his army of 1,000 left Buffalo by water to sail to Chicago. By the time he arrived he had only 200 effective soldiers; he lost the rest to death, illness, and desertion.

New York Governor Enos Throop proclaimed, *"An infinitely wise and just God has seen fit to employ pestilence as one means of scourging the human race for its sins."* Local church and civic leaders called for days of fasting, prayer and humiliation. Writers for the Cabinet suggested laudanum, mustard poultices and bloodletting. The local newspapers were full of ads for all sorts of cholera remedies. A Dr. McLean, *"well known to his fellow citizens"* according to the *Cabinet*, claimed to have a cure for all cases. Happily, I did not find Dr. McLean amongst our membership.

An article in the *Schenectady Union-Star* in 1948, as well as a piece written by Dr. Ellis Kellert, reported that the city fathers opened a cholera hospital using some rooms in the old brick college building; however, according to the Cabinet, the original resolution authorizing the rooms specifically stated that they were not to be used as a cholera hospital. More likely, they were used as office space for Dr. Tonnelier (see below). As further support for the absence of a cholera hospital in Schenectady, the weekly health summary of August 12, 1834 reported that Mrs. Snell of Ferry St. died at a hospital "out of the city."

During that same week, 4 other Schenectadians died, including *"Jenny Fonda, a colored women, aged 70."* There were also 3 victims in Rotterdam, one man on a canal boat, 45 in Albany and 106 in NYC. Because of the outbreak, Union College sent its students home before Commencement. Although it is difficult to estimate a death toll, dozens—perhaps even a few hundred—may have died. And, Schenectady was still a small town at that time, so it is likely that our entire community was grieving. Funerals were held almost hourly. The epidemic ended with an early September cold wave; cholera bacteria can't survive temperatures below 51°F.

Medical Society charter members who fought the cholera included Dr. John Tonnelier, who had been appointed City Physician in 1826 at an annual salary of $75. The Board of Health required all residents to report cases of cholera to him by ten o'clock in the morning. Dr. Tonnelier examined the crews of canal boats passing through and prohibited any boat with cholera on board from docking; his duties also included providing smallpox vaccinations and treating the poor. The office of City Physician had been established in about 1818 by the Common Council.

We take pride that our city fathers showed concern for the poor 150 years before Medicaid. (Was this the beginning of socialized medicine?) At their meeting of August 6, 1832 the Board of Health stated, "all physicians of this city are employed by the Board of Health to attend upon those who do not feel able to pay for medical services." The medical records of Dr. McDougall contained the names of the patients treated, the drugs provided and the bills for his services. All patients were treated equitably, regardless of their ability to pay. These patients included Robert Ellis, Major Sneed and Lucas, the canal boy. Among the drugs he used were opium, calomel, quinine, bicarbonate of soda, gargle of myrrah, kino and Haust anodyne. Therapies included bleeding and cupping!

Drs. Daniel Toll (who came out of retirement), J. C. Magoffin and Benjamin Franklin Joslin—all founding members of our Society—also treated cholera patients. Dr. Joslin was serving as Professor of Natural Philosophy at Union College in 1834; during the epidemic, he performed original research on the disease. The following year, he presented his results at the meeting of the NYS Medical Society. His paper, entitled *The Physiology of Respiration and the Chemistry of the Blood Applied to Epidemic Cholera*" correlated an elevation of the dew point with lowered barometric pressure during the epidemic.

Dr. Joslin was an interesting character. His signature clearly appears in the original minutes, but history records his birth in 1796 which would have made him only fourteen years old at that time of the Society's founding. He graduated from Union in 1821 and received his medical degree from Columbia University in 1826. (Remember, most physicians at the time did not attend medical school, so it was possible to receive formal medical education even after acquiring a license). While practicing in Schenectady, he performed cupping and bleeding. Later, he moved to NYC and practiced homeopathy, later writing a textbook on the subject in 1850.

Cholera visited our city several times after the 1834 epidemic. In 1849, we had twelve cases and four deaths. A temporary hospital was established to care for the victims. On September 6th, President Zachary Taylor came through Schenectady after having contracted cholera in Erie, Pennsylvania. The *Schenectady Reflector* reported *"a large concourse of citizens were at the railroad department but few of whom could get a sight of him. The General we understand was continuing to regain his health, but was so feeble that he did not leave his car."*

Dr. Ellis Kellert noted that a potential prevention, and a treatment, for cholera were available here but not actually used. In 1832, Professor Chester Averill, of Union College, noted the connection between cholera and drinking water and published a paper suggesting that chloride of lime should be added to drinking water as a disinfectant. But, his advice was ignored for many years. Albany physician, Dr. James McNaughton (later a President of the Albany County Medical Society) treated 4 cholera patients with transfusions of water, salt, and subcarbonate of soda, but then decided it was not worthwhile. It is unfortunate that lime, as a disinfectant for drinking water, and hydration, as a treatment for cholera, were not adopted sooner; these treatments eventually were recognized as medical breakthroughs that saved countless lives.

In 1885, Dr. Robert Koch of Hanover, Germany identified the Vibrio bacteria as the cause of cholera. Antibiotics and hydration are the treatments used today. Cholera still causes illness and death following natural disasters and in underdeveloped areas. Dr. Koch won the Nobel Prize for Medicine or Physiology in 1905 for his work with tuberculosis.

Typhoid Fever

The first contagious disease mentioned in our minutes is typhoid fever. Typhoid is caused by a Salmonella bacterium and causes fever, abdominal pain and diarrhea. It is spread in contaminated water. In previous times it was noted that typhoid and other diseases occurred where large groups of people congregated, especially near swampy water. The impact of the disease on the residents of Schenectady in the 19th century is illustrated by the action of the Union College Board of Trustees in 1807, which resolved:

"no student between the months of June and November may go anywhere upon the flats south of State Street or upon the bank of the Mohawk or bathe in the river."

Fire hydrants became available in Schenectady in 1872. The water was contaminated and typhoid was prevalent. By 1884, the Medical Society began demanding that the city fathers improve our local water supply. In 1897, the Rotterdam Wells became our primary source, replacing private wells and the Mohawk River. This change had a dramatic impact. During the last 6 months of 1896 there were 61 cases., compared with only 17 in the first 9 months of 1897.

The sanitation at Union improved substantially, prompting President Raymond to declare in 1899, *"In the past so much has been said of the dangers facing young men coming to Union College, and the frequent appearance of typhoid among them."* The quality of our water quality from the Rotterdam Wells was considered to be the best in the State.

Despite the marked decrease in typhoid fever, it did stay with us a while longer. In 1917, for example, 37 patients with typhoid were admitted to Ellis, 5 of whom died. Today, there are about 40 cases of typhoid yearly in NYS, almost all resulting from foreign travel.

In the latter part of the 20th century, our Society again expressed concern about the water supply. Our President, Dr. Farlin, along with Dr. Thomas Oram, Ellis Pathologist and Chair of the Environmental Health Committee, wrote to the Town of Rotterdam Supervisor requesting information on any possible impact the new shopping mall could have on the aquifer. Dr. Oram and Dr. Carl George, Professor of Biology at Union College, obtained samples from the Poentic Creek, which flows near the aquifer, and from 2 similar creeks in Pattersonville and Oppenheim. These were sent to the Museum of Natural History in NYC where the Curator of Ichthyology discovered that creek chubs from the Rotterdam samples had striking abnormalities in their nostrils and caudal fins. The DOH denied their request to perform further testing, and the mall was built.

Diphtheria

Diphtheria is predominantly a childhood infection caused by Corynebacteria. It is basically an upper airway disease and patients may suffocate when their trachea and larynx become blocked with thick mucus.

The Society informed its members at the March 1897 meeting that all specimens for diphtheria will be screened free of charge. In Schenectady, this was mostly an outpatient disease because Ellis Hospital, in accordance with its bylaws, did not allow these highly contagious patients to be admitted to the hospital.

In 1902, the Society resolved to continue quarantine of diphtheria houses until the patient's temperature was normal for at least 5 days and "throat products" were absent. The Ellis Board of Managers called a special meeting on Feb 2, during a diphtheria epidemic, to "consider the grave condition in which the hospital is placed by reason of the nine cases which are there." Ellis closed the hospital to admissions and asked the City to pay for the treatment of the 9 diphtheria patients already hospitalized. Their diagnosis had not been made until after they were admitted.

In response, the Mayor and the Board of Health established a temporary hospital, complete with an operating room, in the Police Court of City Hall. Heavy canvas partitioned the large room into separate areas for the patients, doctors and nurses. A policeman was stationed outside to enforce the quarantine. Ellis offered to provide care for patients in this temporary "Hospital for Contagious Disease" but still received much criticism in the city newspapers for not admitting diphtheria patients.

The following year, the Medical Society petitioned the Mayor and the Board of Health in October for the establishment of a contagious disease hospital, and the Mayor referred the matter to the Common Council. However, at the November 1908 meeting, the Medical Society remained opposed to the establishment of a contagious disease pavilion in connection with Ellis.

The disease remained prevalent for several decades. For example, in 1918, the Contagious Nurse of the City Bureau of Health visited the homes of 145 patients with diphtheria. Continuing our attempt to understand this serious illness, diphtheria was a frequent topic at our meetings. Once, a member even exhibited a specimen coughed up by a patient. In the 1920s, there were up to 200,000 cases and 15,000 fatalities in the United States.

Around this time, the Schick test became available to diagnose diphtheria. It initially caused controversy among Medical Society members, and in April 1922, the Society voted unanimously against using the test on school children. After an outcry in the press and a lecture to our Society membership by an expert consultant from NYC, we reversed this decision at the June meeting. Eventually a vaccine was developed and diphtheria is now preventable.

Spanish Flu

The Spanish Flu of 1918 was the worst epidemic to visit Schenectady. World War I was raging and there were 24,000 men and women working around-the-clock at General Electric (GE) and 8,000 more at American Locomotive (ALCO). Many lived in crowded conditions. Some 15,000 became ill and 500 died. The United States lost 650,000 out of a population of 189 million. Schenectady ran out of hospital beds and nurses. Schools and theaters were closed and there were no public gatherings. Funeral attendance was limited to next of kin. Funeral directors even ran out of manufactured coffins and they were obliged to make their own.

Of 115 doctors practicing in Schenectady at that time, 19 were serving in the armed forces along with many local nurses. Clearly, the medical community was short-handed. None of our Medical Society members lost their lives in the epidemic although one physician, who was sent from AMC to help us, caught the flu and died after working only one week in Schenectady. Physicians Hospital on Union Street (page 31) reopened under the new name of Emergency Hospital and its 30 beds were staffed by AMC students, under the supervision of the Head Nurse from Ellis. Since all schools were closed, teachers were recruited to work as nurses and given a one-day training course.

Dr. Ward Stone, the Ellis pathologist, constituted a vaccine from sputum specimens and carried out a controlled trial with the "pupil nurses." The results showed that the vaccinated students had a much lower rate of flu compared to the controls. General Electric requested the vaccine for its employees. Years later, Dr. Oram was unable to explain why Dr. Stone's flu vaccine could have been effective because the sputum was boiled for such a long time, the heat should have destroyed any antigenic material.

The records of the autumn meetings of the Schenectady County Medical Society report scientific discussions on the "so-called flu." (The quotation marks were written in the minutes.) Our doctors were not certain that this actually was influenza, because it had always been a much milder disease. In 1918, viruses had not yet been described. The epidemic ended somewhat abruptly on November 11th, coincidentally the same day as the War ended. The severe toll of the Spanish Flu on Schenectady was duly noted by our present-day County Health Department, which took all necessary precautions to protect our residents from the H1N1 flu pandemic of 2009.

Other Public Health Functions

In addition to the contagious diseases, the Medical Society as a whole, or through its committees, played an active role in the public health of our County.

Some activities occurred on an annual basis, such as the Diabetic Clinic conducted by Dr. Zaia, which in 1957 alone screened 5,330 people, of whom 135 tested positive. The Heart Kitchen, which was located at City Hospital, was sponsored by the Heart Committee and provided healthy cooking classes to all Schenectady residents. In 1958, 82 of our members served at least 4 hours each at the Red Cross blood drives, during which 5,786 units were collected.

That same year, members volunteered to staff a polio clinic for those who had not yet received their Salk vaccine. Dr. John Kennedy Sr. sponsored a glaucoma-screening day in 1960 at a local public school during which all attendees could have their intraocular pressures checked by an ophthalmologist. In 1967, the Society approved a pilot project for markedly obese children in the Schenectady City public schools.

In 1971, our urologists and primary care physicians endorsed the County Veneral Disease (VD) clinic, after our Public Health Committee survey found that VD in the County was under-diagnosed and undertreated. At the April 1970 meeting, we unanimously voted for a mass rubella clinic for all children up to 10 years of age, reversing a Comitia Minora recommendation to restrict the clinic to only indigent children.

The public health of our community continues to be a major concern for the Medical Society today.

Physicians Hospital

MEDICAL EDUCATION

Student and Post-Graduate Training

Schenectady physicians realized the importance of medical education at least a decade before our Society existed. The consistory minutes of the Dutch Church on October 25, 1799 record the following:

"A complaint having been delivered in against Gysbert Van Slice, the Sexton, that he delivered the scull (sic) of a corpse to the house of Dr Anderson; being sent for and interrogated, he finally confessed that he had taken a scull [sic] out of the burying yard and delivered it to Mr. Hagaman, a student of medicine with Dr. Anderson (who became our first Vice-President eleven years later)."

Over the years, the Schenectady hospitals and many Schenectady physicians have had rotations for medical students. In addition, most of the Schenectady hospitals had internships. Dr. Richard Woodruff, born in China to missionary parents, graduated from AMC in 1913. He interned at Mercy Hospital on Union St. and later became Chief of Surgery at Ellis. (There was another surgeon with the same name a generation later.) Dr. Joseph Capritta graduated from AMC in 1937 and interned at Schenectady City Hospital on Altamont Avenue. Ellis and St. Clare's had their own residency programs, and Sunnyview had orthopedic residents from the Mayo Clinic (including Drs. Holmblad and Nelson) and AMC, as well as residents in physical medicine and rehabilitation.

In 1966, two nationally known medical educators visited Schenectady for a survey of post-graduate education resources. Their conclusion was disappointing:

"insufficient evidence in teaching and even in learning… philosophy here was archaic… when I was an intern…sense of chauvinism in the individual hospitals… few medical men locally have gone on to get their boards and few do critical evaluation of patient care… lack of communication between hospitals… small corps of men interested in education."

They also opined that Glenridge Hospital and Sunnyview were not included in the teaching. Nevertheless, Dr. Tischler, an obstetrician-gynecologist, made a valiant attempt to integrate the hospitals and improve teaching. He worked very hard to achieve this, spending thousands of hours at meetings for more than four years!

In May 1967, Dr. Tischler reported on a Proposed Governing Structure for Schenectady Affiliated Hospitals Medical Education Program, including details of qualifications and responsibilities for Executive Faculty. In January 1969, he recruited Mr. William Golub to join the Board of Directors of the Education Program as a community member. Each of the 5 hospitals had 2 representatives, the budget was $50,000, and the committee sought a retired medical school dean to serve as its leader.

However, just 2 months later he reported there was no enthusiasm for the educational program among important segments of the educational community. *"Unless there [is] a change in attitudes, the prognosis for an integrated program is poor."*

In March 1969, he reported to the Society that the medical chiefs of both hospitals had not met. The following year he reported an impasse. And, a year after that, the last mention of the initiative was in the minutes of April 1971:

"It was felt his committee should inquire of St. Clare's officials what their educational plans are after the disbandment of their internship, and how our medical society can assist their educational committee in the future." (How anti-climactic, after FOUR YEARS of meetings!)

In October 1977, our Society received a letter from Dr. Allan Nadler, Founder and Director of the St. Clare's Family Practice Residency, informing us that their Family Health Center was accepting patients. (That helped clarify their plans.) The St. Clare's program was the first family medicine residency sponsored by a community hospital in Upstate New York. Over the past 33 years, there have been nearly 250 graduates, many of whom are practicing in the Capital Region. The program also offers an osteopathic internship for graduates of osteopathic medical schools. Dr. Gary Dunkerley is the current program director.

For several years, AMC had two teams of residents and interns on the medical floors of Ellis as well as in the ICU, and several of those doctors have remained to practice in Schenectady. During that time (while Karl Adler was Chief of Medicine), a survey of the 16 one-month elective rotations offered to AMC medical residents (including those at AMC, St. Peter's and the Veteran's Administration hospitals in Albany, and Ellis) rated our infectious disease elective as first in educational value, thanks to Dr. Rockwell. Rheumatology was number four.

In addition to medicine there have been Ellis residents or rotating residents from AMC in pathology, neurology, and orthopedics. Since the merger of the hospitals, Ellis now sponsors the Family Practice Residency.

Continuing Education

At our founding in 1810, we chose a *"suitable person to attend the Lectures in the City of New York on the different Branches of Medicine."* We know that Schenectady physicians trained apprentices and medical students in their offices because it was stated in the minutes in 1873 that was a misdemeanor to retain a medical student in one's office without presenting a certificate of proper preliminary education and qualifications. And, in 1896, Dr. Kathan moved that *"students ought to pay for the privilege of studying with practitioners."*

In 1873 the Society also approved $25 to purchase medical and surgical journals to be circulated amongst the neighbors. This transaction created the nidus of the Medical Society Library, which became housed at Ellis Hospital many years later. The Society had a Library Committee that purchased new books. In 1936, ownership of the library was transferred to the hospital, so as to satisfy the requirements of the American College of Surgeons. We have continually supported the library over the years, and also donated funds to the St. Clare's Hospital medical library before the hospital was closed as a result of the Berger Commission in 2008. (More on that, later.)

Our Society encouraged its members to take continuing education very seriously. Each physician was expected to present a scientific talk each year, and if he missed his turn, he was fined twenty dollars. There were usually three or four such talks at each meeting and, until about 1936, they took place at the beginning of the meeting, before the business portion. From the rebirth of our Society in 1870 until just before World War II, almost all of these lectures were given by our members.

Sometimes, the Society held debates instead of lectures. In 1893, *"after a lively debate the society decided that laxative treatment was the best in inflammatory conditions of the appendix."* For the next meeting, the topic was "Resolved that alcohol is not necessary in medicine." (Almost a century later Dr. Charles Smith and Dr. Ritterband debated Dr. Spring and Dr. Gelfand on "Cognitive vs Surgical Reimbursement.")

For many years, the Secretary mailed post cards to the members announcing the meeting date and place, and listing the various speakers and their topics. The minutes recorded the names of those who participated in each discussion and, frequently, there were many who spoke. In February 1897, a paper was presented on retention and extraction of the placenta and nearly 20 members participated in the discussion. We can conclude from this that a large number of members included obstetrics in their medical practice.

Over the past 140 years there have been hundreds of papers presented by our members. Here are some examples:

1875 - 2 cases of embolus and a tracheotomy

1879 - a method for detection for salicylic acid as an adulterant in beer

1897 - formalin as the anti-septic of the future

1898 - Dr. Clowe showed X-ray pictures of fractures of both bones of the forearm; copper poisoning at the General Electric Plant

1901 - serum therapy; septicemia

1902 - pneumonia in children; intestinal obstruction

1905 - photos of chest showing TB deposits

1906 - dangers of ether and chloroform anesthesia, and methods of lessening them

1908 - acute articulator rheumatism; simple glaucoma,

1909 - hydrophobia in man, rabies in dogs, and dog muzzles

1911 - treatment of pneumonia based on the the elimination of NaCl by Dr. Kathan

1914 - recent advances in cancer research; a review of 1,000 obstetrical cases in private practice

1915 - infection and immunity by Dr. Ward Stone

1922 - General Electric Company film of an orthopedic operation

1923 - insulin treatment of diabetes; 50 cases of syphilis

1930 - Saratoga as a health resort, the medical value of the mineral waters; demonstration of a new portable EKG (electrocardiogram) machine by the General Electric Company

1933 - the Research Laboratory used a new cast cutter, which they invented to remove a lower leg cast, based on the principle of the can opener,

1934 - General Electric Physicist and Nobel Prize Winner Irving Langmueir explained the Einstein Theory of Relativity

In 1934 we sponsored a clinical day at Ellis Hospital followed by lunch, at which our members presented 14 scientific papers. As the years passed however, the Society increasingly turned to outside speakers for education. From 1927 through 1945, 164 speakers presented papers, only 44 of whom were members.

This change was lamented by Dr. Ellis Kellert, long-time Ellis pathologist and medical historian, who wrote in 1945: *"In the years to come, when some historian will survey the society proceedings, it will seem as though our membership contributed very little scientifically in this period."* Perhaps this reflects that science marches on and opportunities for an individual practitioner to make scientific contributions are limited.

After World War II many of our speakers were top medical authorities in the United States. In 1952, we had Dr. Russell Cecil (Editor of the *"Textbook of Medicine"* and Professor at Cornell University Medical School) speak on pneumonia. Dr. Wolf (of the Wolf-Parkinson-White

Syndrome) spoke on the EKG and chest pain. Others included Dr. Smith-Petersen (Orthopedist—remember his nail?), Dr. Crohn (of the disease by the same name), Dr. Milton Halpern (NYC Medical Examiner) and Dr. Arthur Masters (of 2-step test fame). Dr. Copeland (Georgetown University) spoke on breast cancer, Dr. Morris Fishbein (editor of *JAMA*) spoke about the future of medicine and predicted euthanasia, and Dr. Gerald Parkhurst invited Dr. George Papanicolaou (of the Pap test) to Schenectady.

Another interesting program was in October 1961 when the Director of the Office of Medical Defense of the NYS DOH spoke about atomic bomb attacks. He advised that we should remain in our shelters for 48 hours after the last bomb, and radiation monitors would notify the public when it was safe. However, he did not have a satisfactory answer for how to respond if strangers crowded into a shelter and displaced its owner.

In May 1967, Dr. Joseph Molner, a nationally known syndicated medical columnist, spoke on the responsibility of writing his type of column. He stressed avoidance of controversial subjects! What wasn't controversial at that time was that meeting attendance suffered with a scientific topic on the program so Dr. Penta, the retiring program chairman, said that his successor would include non-scientific topics as well.

In January 1967, the Continuing Education Committee recommended that the County Society discontinue scientific sessions at the regular meetings. Instead, these would be conducted by the local hospitals and the Society would strongly support such efforts. This was inevitable due to increasing specialization. However, there were still occasional scientific programs presented by local physicians. In October 1977, Dr. Robert Cassidy (Society President) asked Dr. Strosberg to speak on "Immunology for Real Doctors" at the Edison Club. Dr. Parkhurst kindly prepared the 35mm slides and—without the speaker's knowledge and much to his chagrin—added an image of a scantily clad woman sitting on a bar stool. Several years later, Dr. Rockwell spoke about AIDS and, in 2009, Dr David Pratt (Schenectady County Health Commissioner) spoke on H1N1 influenza.

ELLIS CLINIC DISPUTE

At its January 2010 Gala, the Ellis Hospital Foundation honored our Medical Society on the occasion of our Bicentennial Anniversary. However, the relationship between our organizations was not always so cordial.

At our October 1899 meeting, it *"was moved and seconded that a committee of three be appointed by the President to draw up a resolution to be presented to the Board of Managers of Ellis Hospital in regards to the abuse of charity existing in that institution, abuse of the dispensary of Ellis Hospital by many persons who can well afford to pay for their treatment, to the deterrence not only to the members of the society but to the hospital as well, greatly increasing the expenses..."* (In other words, freeloaders!) At that time, Ellis was a 30-bed hospital on Jay Street.

Apparently, in that era, our Society did not have much influence with Ellis Hospital. At the September 1901 meeting, the Committee on the Dispensary reported that the hospital authorities had ignored our communication. The committee finally met with the Board of Managers the following month to discuss "hospital abuses."

The Board of Managers told the committee that *"General Electric and ALCO threatened to stop their annual contributions toward the maintenance of the hospital should the law relating to the dispensary be enforced."* These contributions amounted to about $4000. The Medical Society backed down, and the "abuse" continued.

Although the Society requested physician representation in the management of Ellis as early as 1908, it wasn't until 1971 that physicians were appointed to the Board of Ellis (and St. Clare's). However, the Society minutes are not clear on this point. In the early minutes of the Schenectady Dispensary, there were at least two physicians listed on the Board of Managers, one being Dr. Kathan. (There have been four generations of Dr. Kathans who became physicians.)

Charitably, the Society did not hold a grudge, and in 1937 our 110 members pledged $24,000 to the Ellis Building Fund. Only two years later, we found that the meeting room in the newly constructed hospital was inadequate for our needs and the Sunnyview Board of Trustees invited us to meet there. Sunnyview had sufficient space to accommodate us and they agreed to provide *"a girl to answer the phone."* When the Ellis Board learned that the county Medical Society might meet permanently outside the grounds of Ellis Hospital, they asked for a special meeting at which they offered us use of the School of Nursing auditorium. They also committed to make any necessary repairs and accommodations for Society meetings.

HEALTH INSURANCE

The physicians of generations past would be very surprised to learn about group practices, hospitalists, advertisements, osteopaths, international medical graduates, physician assistants, and—most of all—Medicare, private health insurance and HMOs. Soon after the turn of the 20th century, there was strong opposition to employer-provided compulsory health insurance in NYS. In part, this may have arisen from our members' reactions to the Socialist Party victory in the 1911 local elections, when Schenectady elected a mayor, 8 aldermen, 8 supervisors, a state assemblyman, and a Common Council president, all from the Socialist Party

The first mention of opposition to the NYS compulsory health insurance law for poor people was in the April 1916 minutes. We received letters from other county societies (including Cortland, Kings, New York, Albany and Herkimer) asking our support to fight the proposed legislation. The original documents remain on file in our office. The anti-health insurance forces grew in number and, at the September 1919 meeting, our Society resolved to unite with *"dentists, nurses, [and] druggists for protective organization against health insurance."* Later that year, the health insurance law passed the State Senate, but was defeated in the Assembly. The Russian Revolution a year earlier, and the rise of socialist governments in Europe probably contributed to the anti-health insurance fervor. By that time, Germany already had government-supported medical care.

It is interesting to follow the evolution of opinion of our members about health insurance over the decades. Our leaders worked closely with Blue Cross/Blue Shield, General Electric and Workers' Compensation, and we are proud that they were able to break through philosophical barriers into uncharted waters of medical economics. One might surmise that they would have welcomed Medicaid, however, because they did take care of the poor for free. In 1933, at the height of the Great Depression, our predecessors performed 200,000 "free calls," including office visits, house calls, hospital rounds, and clinic visits.

Fifty years later, in 1983, our Society was instrumental in the formation of MVP Health Plan, under the leadership of Dr. Richard Lange. This initiative arose from the belief that a physician-friendly health plan would be a model for success. More recently, in 2007, our Society voted against a resolution to endorse national health insurance. However, during the debate over health insurance reform in 2010, there was considerable controversy about its merits—locally and within the State Society and the AMA.

SOCIAL GOOD

Our Society has a long history of philanthropy. In 1906, we donated $50 in cash to the San Francisco Earthquake Relief Fund and sent medical books and instruments to our colleagues in California. After World War II, the Women's Auxiliary (now, the Alliance to the Medical Society) collected medication samples from our offices to send to war-torn Europe, and they later assisted Dr. Arthur Penta with collection of samples and supplies for his medical missionary work in Latin America.

Our Society has always been supportive of medical education. Our biggest charitable achievement has been our Philanthropic Trust Fund, which has awarded hundreds of thousands of dollars to more than one hundred medical students from Schenectady County. In addition, we have sponsored a pre-medical scholarship at Union College for a student from Schenectady and at least four of these recipients have gone on to medical school, eventually returning home to practice and join the Society that assisted with their undergraduate education.

For many years, we sponsored a full scholarship at the Ellis Hospital School of Nursing (tuition in 1951 was $350) and in 1949, we gave $200 for a jukebox for the student nurses' lounge and another $129 for records for the juke box. In 1951, we donated $200 for the Peoples' Free Blood Bank and $100 to the Mayor's Committee for gift kits to soldiers leaving town for the Korean War.

The Society had its own division of the Community Chest and, later on, the United Fund. It was common for us to exceed our fund-raising quotas. We donated regularly to the Schenectady Health Care Issues Committee, which we co-sponsor, and to public information campaigns such as anti-smoking programs and the Health Care Proxy Initiative.

In 1981, the Society donated $5,000 to a fund established to save Proctors Theatre, on State Street. More recently, it has been our policy to encourage members to donate as individuals to the charities and causes which we deem worthwhile.

Perhaps more important than monetary donations are contributions of time. As noted, at the height of the Great Depression in 1933, the Society provided 205,000 "free calls" for the poor. These included 56,000 office visits, 67,000 house calls, 14,000 Ellis Dispensary visits, 31,000 admissions to Ellis, 22,000 City Dispensary visits, 8000 visits to city physicians and 7000 charity calls at City Hospital.

In addition, the doctors of the Society performed thousands of physical examinations for the Boys' Club, the Girls' Club and Carver Community Center throughout several decades. These acts of charity enabled these children, most of whom were indigent, to attend summer camps. At that time, there was no Medicaid program. The entire list of names of who participated in the above activities is too long to print, but included among them were Drs. Tepper, Henderson, Purcell, Veeder, Farlin, Cunningham, Lange, Tytko, Vlahides, Busino, Sr., Best, and Vacca.

Dozens of our members attended Red Cross blood donations, which were held throughout the years, at a time when physician presence was required. In 1958, for example, the Red Cross held 41 "bleeding days," during which 82 doctors served at least 4 hours each and 5,786 units of blood were collected and distributed to area hospitals.

In 1964, Dr. Arnold Ritterband and Dr. Jack Sheridan directed a training program at St. Clare's for 120 ambulance drivers and crews from 17 ambulance companies, including some from Albany, Rensselaer and Saratoga Counties. Dr. James Holmblad and Dr. Gerald Haines also participated. Topics included cardiac resuscitation, control of bleeding, splinting of fractures, oxygen administration, chest injuries, burns, and obstetrics.

Our members sat on the advisory board of the Practical Nursing Program, which started at Nott Terrace High School in 1952 and was joined by Mt. Pleasant High School in 1963. This was the first high school practical nursing program in NYS, and it was later adopted by other school districts. The graduates almost always passed their Boards and many obtained positions at the Schenectady hospitals.

MUTUAL AID

An important function of any professional society is to come to the aid of its members in their time of need, and our Society also fulfilled this function on occasion.

Narcotics

For many years, the sale of narcotics in the United States was not regulated. For example, in the mid-1890s, the Sears, Roebuck and Co. Catalog advertised a syringe containing a small amount of cocaine for $1.50.

It was not until 1914 that Congress passed the Harrison Narcotic Act, introduced by the Hon. Francis Burton Harrison of NYS, which regulated opiates. The provisions of this act were complicated and difficult to understand. The State of New York also had a Department of Narcotic Drug Control, which, according to our minutes of January 1921, *"[was] absolutely unnecessary and a waste of money, and a great annoyance and should be abolished."*

In 1924, two of our most prominent members, Dr. Byrant and Dr. Keigher, were arrested on a minor, technical violation of the Harrison Act. On the unwise advice of their attorney, they both pleaded guilty to the charge. However, their crime was a felony and their licenses to practice medicine were revoked. At the December meeting, our members assessed themselves $25.00 each to provide a legal defense fund for their colleagues.

Our Society contacted United States Senator Wadsworth and Congressman Crowther and, with their help, a presidential pardon from Calvin Coolidge was obtained. This resulted in reinstatement of their licenses.

Privileges

Another example of the Society providing assistance to its members was recorded in the December 1953 minutes, when we voted to send a letter to the Board of Managers of Ellis regretting the revocation of general practitioners' (GP) surgical privileges without cause, and requested reconsideration. After the motion passed, Dr. MacMillan, Chief of Surgery, requested the floor in order to speak on behalf of the Medical Board of Ellis Hospital, but he was ruled out of order as the motion had already passed. (This was not a cordial meeting!)

At the next meeting in February 1954, our Society endorsed a letter from the Schenectady County Academy of General Practice, pointing out that none of the doctors were given notice of the revocation of privileges, or an opportunity to present their defense. The reasons cited by Ellis were poor attendance at department meetings and low surgical volume. However, the general practitioners pointed out that 75% of the surgical staff had poor meeting attendance and, on many occasions, the GPs were unable to schedule their surgery at Ellis because beds were unavailable and they were forced to take their patients elsewhere.

Malpractice

In 1979, our society contributed $2,000 to help defray the legal expenses of Dr. Eugene Drago in a lawsuit brought against him by a Troy attorney. Dr. Drago had been sued for malpractice solely because his name was printed on an EKG form; he had no professional relationship with the patient. Even when this was explained to the attorney, he refused to drop Dr. Drago from the lawsuit. After he ultimately won his malpractice case, Dr. Drago counter-sued the attorney. His case almost made it to the United States Supreme Court, but Associate Justice Thurgood Marshall declined to hear it.

MILK COMMITTEE

The month of August 1906 was a very sad time for the parents of Schenectady. Forty-eight children under five yeas of age died, mostly from gastrointestinal diseases. Dr. Clute, the City Health Officer, attributed the deaths to impure, unrefrigerated milk. This tragedy sparked the formation of the Medical Society Milk Committee, which functioned for about 30 years. The Committee, whose ad hoc members included the City Chemist and City Milk Inspector, was responsible for certifying all milk sold in the County. In fact, the top of each milk bottle carried our seal of approval.

The dairymen were sometimes invited to attend our meetings to help develop appropriate policies. In April 1910, the Committee certified the milk of St. John's Dairy. The treasurer's record book for 1910 notes a deposit of $15.00 from Gold Seal Dairy, and a payment to Dr. Ward Stone (Ellis Pathologist) for examination of the milk. Analysis showed that Borden's milk fat content averaged 3.8 % in seven specimens (range 2.8%to 4.5%).

The doctors on the Milk Committee actually visited dairies to check on TB testing of cows and bacteria counts in the milk. In October 1913, a count of 4,000 was recorded in the minutes. In 1914, 2 doctors on the Milk Committee traveled to Canajoharie to inspect the Gold Seal herd. At a joint meeting with the Montgomery County Medical Society in March 1919, the program was "Milk Production, Old and New, Illustrated with Stereoptics [sic]."

Dr. Joseph Garlick, an AMC graduate who was to become our president in 1930, also served as Health Commissioner. He was a pioneer in pasteurization and, from 1916 to 1918 our first-year infant mortality declined 50%, from 164 to 81 deaths per thousand. Dr. Garlick also eliminated the sale of loose milk and Grade C milk. (Does loose milk come from loose cows?)

Our Milk Committee was a member of the American Association of Medical Milk Commissions, for which our membership paid $25 in annual dues. In 1917, our entire Society was invited to inspect a new milk production plant in Glenville. At the Annual Meeting in 1935, Dr. York, the retiring president, delivered the scientific talk entitled "Milk: A Review of the Literature, its Uses and Abuses." In 1936 the Milk Committee showed a motion picture of milk production and reported that we were getting good service from a farm in Bennington, Vermont that produced certified milk.

Nothing more is heard about milk until April 1973, when Dr. Staunton reported that the Department of Agriculture would assume milk inspection for the Health Department. Our Auxiliary was concerned about this and Dr. Staunton *"mentioned cogent reasons why that change would not be desirable."* Unfortunately, the secretary did not record his cogent reasons in the minutes.

In 1976, the Crowley Dairy wanted our home addresses so we could receive a sample of their new product, which blended *Lactobacillus acidophilus* cultures with 2% milk. The Society would not release our addresses so we never received the free milk.

WORLD WAR I

The Great War first appears in our minutes in June 1916. Our Society was asked to march in a Preparedness Parade and furnish a band. The following year, a representative of the Army Surgeon General attended a meeting to request aid in examining potential recruits and to solicit physicians to join the service.

We can be very proud of the patriotism shown by our predecessors. Our Society voted *"...to work in conjunction with the recruitment committee, to remove as far as possible, disqualifying defects in rejected applicants for Army or Navy... and treat dependent families of all enlisted men without charge."* And, in a show of support for the doctors who enlisted, we resolved that *"...men who stay at home take care of the practices of those doctors who [go] to the front and turn over proceeds to their families."*

The Society also purchased a service flag with 19 stars, one for each member serving with the armed forces, and the Honor Roll of their names was read at each meeting.

During the War years, the American public was requested not to drive their cars on Sunday in order to help conserve the national supply of gasoline. At the October 1918 meeting, our Society suggested that members purchase green crosses to attach to their automobiles in order to identify the driver as a physician, presumably on his way to visit a sick patient. Apparently, several members had reported some looks of disapproval from the public while driving on a Sunday. Fortunately, the War ended the following month. Years later, at the June 1926 meeting, it was reported that osteopaths and dentists were also displaying the green crosses on their cars, and it was suggested that physicians substitute insignia provided by the AMA.

WORLD WAR II

The first of anticipation of World War II appeared in our minutes more than one year prior to Pearl Harbor. At the meeting in October 1940, the Medical Preparedness Committee presented a plan for physicians in military service to select a physician who would cover their practices and remit one-third of all collected fees to the Physician Welfare Supervisory Committee. The Committee, in turn, would transfer the money to the family of the deployed doctor. The telephone company offered to connect phone lines between the doctors' offices free of charge. However, this patriotism was not universal. When a motion was made to waive the dues of departing colleagues, one member objected citing that military officers earned good salaries, and the money was needed to help fight the "socialization of medicine."

In November 1940, Dr. Joe Naumoff, the Secretary of the Society, became the first physician to leave the city for active military service and Dr. Gomer Richards assumed his office.

In February 1941, the Medical Reserve Officers Military District of Schenectady started a weekly "medical school." Dr. Frumkin spoke on communicable diseases; Dr. Runge spoke on organization of medical detachments with infantry, cavalry, and field artillery; and Dr. Korkosz spoke on chemical warfare.

In June 1942, the Society published a notice in the local newspapers asking the public to place all requests for house calls early in the morning. Physicians had to drive their routes in the most efficient manner due to the rationing of gasoline and tires. During the War years, the Society had a Gasoline Grievance Committee to which members could request additional allocations. (At the February 1974 meeting, during the Arab Oil boycott following the Yom Kippur War, our Society sent a resolution to the Federal Energy Office demanding that physicians be allocated sufficient gasoline for their cars.)

As the War continued, and more physicians joined the war effort, our numbers became depleted. At the meeting in December 1942, Dr. Trader reported that the Schenectady War Council was concerned with the large number of local physicians (41) who joined the armed forces. At the meeting in February 1943, Dr. Jameson resolved that no doctor be permitted to leave the area for professional education or study during the emergency. By March, there was also a shortage of nurses. In October, the four housestaff physicians at Ellis (including Dr. Humphrey) joined the Army, and the hospital was left with no medical coverage at night. The

Medical Society discussed provision of in-house coverage at night for a $10 night "honorarium." However, some members thought that Ellis should hire a house physician.

At the March 1945 meeting, a motion was made that the entire Society go en masse to the Red Cross to donate blood. However, this must have been controversial, because that meeting did not adjourn until 11:25 pm. Happily, there is no mention in the minutes of any Member of our society who killed or wounded in action during the war.

In 1948, the Medical Society of the State of New York voted to assess each member $12 to raise a fund of $250,000, which would help pay for the education of the children of those physicians who lost their lives in the war.

FROM OUR CENTENNIAL BOOKLET

The Society's Centenial Celebration in 1910 was a daylong affair, with a Scientific Program in the morning and afternoon, and a gala dinner in the evening at the Edison Hotel. Reproduced here from the Centennial Booklet are the list of members of the Society in 1910, the agenda for the Scientific Program, the dinner menu and the 1910 composite photograph.

Dr. Edwin Young, Glenville.
Dr. Wm. L. Pearson, 713 Union St.
Dr. Geo. E. McDonald, 213 So. Centre St.
Dr. J. L. Schoolcraft, 518 Union St.
Dr. Charles C. Duryee, 31 Barrett St.
Dr. Wm. T. Clute, 520 Liberty St.
Dr. H. V. Mynderse, 225 State St.
Dr. John A. Heatly, 308 So. Centre St.
Dr. J. F. McEncroe, 523 Union St.
Dr. D. L. Kathan, 413 Union St.
Dr. Henry A. Kurth, 608 Union St.
Dr. Chas. C. Briggs, 113 Union St.
Dr. Jos. Raymond, 16 Barrett St.
Dr. C. F. Clowe, 613 Union St.
Dr. Janet Murray, 14 Mynderse St.
Dr. W. W. Goddard, 225 Nott Terrace.
Dr. W. G. B. Hall, 408 Union St.
Dr. A. J. Young, 84 Barrett St.
Dr. R. A. Sauter, 925 State St.
Dr. E. J. Wiencke, 28 Jay St.
Dr. Burton Van Zandt, 901 State St.
Dr. J. H. Collins, 620 State St.
Dr. J. E. Reed, 702 Union St.
Dr. G. V. Johnson, 840 State St.
Dr. G. B. Teames, 945 State St.
Dr. W. L. Fodder, 5 Jay St.
Dr. H. A. Staley, 797 State St.
Dr. Wm. Wilson, 204 Mohawk Ave., Scotia.
Dr. Lester Betts, 821 State St.
Dr. C. G. McMullen, 613 State St.
Dr. C. A. McMinn, 5 Park Place.
Dr. E. T. Rulison, 229 State St.
Dr. F. Vander Bogert, 111 Union St.
Dr. E. S. Vass, 1135 State St.
Dr. A. B. Van Vranken, 410 Union St.
Dr. Peter McPartlon, 7 Park Place.
Dr. H. A. Bryant, 500 Crane St.
Dr. A. S. Fay, 100 Broadway.
Dr. R. Gilmore, 1133 State St.
Dr. W. B. Stone, 415 Union St.
Dr. W. A. Stearns, 306 Crane St.
Dr. S. S. Ham, 947 State St.
Dr. Thomas Carney, 615 State St.
Dr. John Fallon, 932 Albany St.
Dr. M. S. Lord, 230 State St.
Dr. E. H. Jackson, 615 State St.

Dr. L. K. Dugan, 818 State St.
Dr. J. W. Racette, 404 Hulett St.
Dr. F. C. Reed, 812 State St.
Dr. H. Gutmann, 34 Jay St.
Dr. K. S. Clark, 130 Nott Terrace.
Dr. R. B. Hoyt, 839 Union St.
Dr. H. G. Hughes, 826 State St.
Dr. E. Gillette, 414 Union St.
Dr. H. L. Towne, 820 Union St.
Dr. Louis Faust, 19 Jay St.
Dr. Wm. P. Faust, 22 Jay St.
Dr. G. W. Bates, 143 Lafayette St.
Dr. E. D. Mann, Lowell Road.
Dr. G. P. Harran, 401 Union St.
Dr. F. J. MacDonald, 770 State St.
Dr. W. D. Spoor, 168 Lafayette St.
Dr. E. P. Foley, 755 Nott St.
Dr. L. A. Gould, 340 Summit Ave.
Dr. F. E. White, 7½ Westinghouse Place.
Dr. A. Grussner, 781 State St.
Dr. J. G. McNutt, 1203 State St.
Dr. S. J. McNutt, 1203 State St.
Dr. J. M. W. Scott, 707 Union St.
Dr. D. W. Overton, 430 State St.
Dr. P. E. Garlock, 305 Hulett St.
Dr. J. P. Faber, 138 Mohawk Ave.
Dr. J. R. Schermerhorn, 56 Glenwood Blvd.
Dr. C. L. Sicard, 800 Albany St.
Dr. E. MacD. Stanton, 613 State St.
Dr. D. R. Kathan, 621 Union St.
Dr. J. J. O'Brien, 170 Lafayette St.
Dr. N. A. Pashayan, 785 State St.
Dr. J. L. Rathbun, 917 State St.
Dr. J. B. Garlick, 1019 State St.
Dr. A. P. Squire, Rotterdam Junction, N. Y.
Dr. Wm. T. Miller, 706 Albany St.
Dr. J. Rossman, 778 State St.
Dr. A. Samorini, 26 Jay St.
Dr. J. J. Burke, 900 Emmett St.
Dr. R. M. Collie, 704 Union St.
Dr. H. Groesbeck, 1226 State St.
Dr. R. C. Keigher, 358 Summit Ave.
Dr. Wm. C. Treder, Scotia.
Dr. J. J. York, 618 State St.
Dr. C. B. Witter, Lafayette St.

Membership Roster, 1910

Scientific Program

**of the Fourth Annual Meeting of the Fourth District Branch of the New York State
Medical Society, at Mohawk Golf Club, September 27, 1910**

MORNING SESSION—9 A. M.

President's Address - - - - - D. L. Kathan, M. D., Schenectady

Chronic Gastro-Intestinal Disorders in Older Children - - - -
- - - - - - - - Frank Vander Bogert, M. D., Schenectady

Fibroid Uterus Didelphys - - - - James B. Conant, M. D., Amsterdam

The Mineral Waters of Saratoga Springs in the Role of Therapeutic Agents -
- - - - - - - George H. Fish, M. D., Saratoga Springs

Report of a Case of Suppurative Mastoiditis with Involvement of the Lateral
Sinus - - - - - - - F. G. Fielding, M. D., Glens Falls

Report of a Case of Dermoid Cyst - - - - George Lenz, M. D., Gloversville

Diabetes - - - - - - George F. Comstock, M. D., Saratoga Springs

Discussion opened by - - - - Charles G. Briggs, M. D., Schenectady

Tuberculosis in Children - - - - - -
- - - - H. S. Goodall, M. D., Stony Wold Sanatorium, Lake Kushaqua

Discussion opened by - - - - - - Louis Faust, M. D., Schenectady

Subject to be Announced - - - - - Charles C. Trembly, M. D., Saranac Lake

AFTERNOON SESSION—2 P. M.

The Functions of Heart Muscle in Relation to Diagnosis and Therapeutics - -
- - - - - - - - Charles Stover, M. D., Amsterdam

A Brief Resume of the Physiological Actions of the Various Heart Tonics; Their
Uses and Indications - - - - W. B. Melick, M. D., Fort Edward

Symposium on Poliomyolitis

    (a) Etiology and Pathology - - - - - - - - -
- - - - Paul A. Lewis, M. D., Rockefeller Institute, New York City

    (b) Symptomatology and Treatment - Charles F. Clowe, M. D., Schenectady

    (c) Surgical Sequels - - - - - J. B. Garlick, M. D., Schenectady

Discussion opened by - - - - - N. A. Pashayan, M. D., Schenectady

Symposium on Surgery of the Upper Abdomen

    (a) Ulcer of the Stomach and Duodonum - - - - -
- - - - - - Charles G. McMullen, M. D., Schenectady

    (b) The Diagnosis and Treatment of Gall Stones -
- - - - - - Grant C. Madill, M. D., Ogdensburg

    (c) Malignant Diseases of the Upper Abdomen - - - -
- - - - - - William P. Faust, M. D., Schenectady

    (d) End Results in Gall Bladder Surgery - - - -
- - - - - - E. MacD. Stanton, M. D., Schenectady

Discussion opened by - - - - D. C. Moriarta, M. D., Saratoga Springs

Scientific Program agenda, 1910

Menu

❦

Blue Points on Half Shell

Sliced Tomatoes   Celery   Olives

Cream of Chicken Supreme

Medallion of Halibut, Sauce Modern

Pommes de Terre, Solferino

Fillet of Beef with Mushrooms

Sweet Potatoes, Saucre

Roman Punch

Broiled Spring Chicken

Green Peas   Mashed Potatoes

Fresh Lobster Salad

Caramel Ice Cream

Chocolate Cake   Sponge Cake   Angel Food

Oranges   Grapes   Bananas

Cheese   Saltines

Coffee

Dinner menu, centennial gala, 1910

Composite photograph of membership, 1910

Our Society celebrated its sesquicentennial on June 2, 1960 at the Edison Club in Scotia. The menu in the gala program was printed in French. Mayor Ellis of Schenectady and the President of MSSNY were among the guests who offered greetings. The keynote speaker was Dr. Ellis Kellert, who spoke on Medical Memorabilia in Old Schenectady. The Doctors' String Quartet provided musical entertainment. After dinner, there was an exhibit in the lobby featuring Doctors' Hobbies, including Dr. Breault's sword canes, Dr. Clowe's stage dancing, Dr. Haines' string quartet, Dr. Holmbald's travel itineraries and Dr. Lange's color photograpy. Other notable physicians who were members at that time included Drs. Cassidy, Cirincione, Drago, Henderson, Jamseson, Mele, Ritterband, Tepper and Sandroni.

*   *   *

The section entitled "Schenectady City Hospital" was written by Elizabeth K. Perkins, RN, who was director of the hospital. Also known as Pest House, Isolation Hospital and Detention Hospital, it was located on Altamont Avenue at the present site of The Avenue Nursing Home (formerly Hallmark Nursing Center). It served various needs through the years, from its opening in 1906 until it closed in the 1960s. At that time, its rehabilitation services were transferred to Sunnyview. The author of "Public Health in Schenectady County" was not identified in the booklet.

The Schenectady City Hospital

Schenectady Rehabilitation and Day Hospital is a Bureau of the Department of Health. Its function is to provide services pertinent to the Public Health of the community. The Hospital dates back to 1906 when, through the effort of Dr. Charles Duryee and Dr. William Chute, a small one-story frame structure was built to serve as a place for the care of smallpox and other contagious disease victims. It was known in the community as the Pest House. In 1910 Dr. Charles Clowe succeeded in adding a somewhat larger brick constructed building. The name was changed to that of Isolation Hospital.

With the new concepts in the treatment of contagious diseases and the farsightedness and persistent efforts of Dr. John H. Collins, a modern addition was built in 1926 with accommodations for 35 to 50 patients. This was then called City Hospital. The medical staff of the hospital was organized shortly thereafter with Dr. Harry Reynolds serving as its first president. From this time until 1951, the hospital served as Schenectady's guardian against epidemics and as a Polio Respirator Center. A Bronchoscopic Clinic was organized and directed by Arthur Q. Penta. This clinic was the first in the northeastern part of the country.

With the decline of contagious diseases and at the request of the Schenectady County Medical Society, Dr. Malcolm Bouton and the medical staff planned and directed the establishment of a Rehabilitation Center for Adults, which was completed in 1951. The ever-increasing number of Geriatric patients in the community needing rehabilitation services resulted in a Pilot Program of Day Hospital, supported in part by New York State Health Department.

The Patient spends the day in the hospital but sleeps home at night. This program has been in existence since October 1956.

The year of 1960 finds the hospital with its present function defined in its new name, "Schenectady Rehabilitation and Day Hospital."

Public Health In Schenectady County

The first mention of a City Physician appeared in the Common Council Minutes of the years 1818 and 1821, authorizing the appointment of such a physician to serve at the pleasure of the Council. It was his duty to attend the sick paupers of the city who were not in alms houses, and to administer to them and their families such medical assistance as they might need. The City Physician was further instructed to keep himself supplied with either genuine kine pock matter or small pox matter for the purpose of inoculating said paupers or any members of their families whenever he felt such inoculation was indicated.

An outbreak of Asiatic cholera, which had spread to Schenectady from Montreal and Quebec, was the occasion for the formation of the first Board of Health in 1832. It was the duty of the City Physician to report back to this board all cases of cholera occurring in the city each morning before ten o'clock. An inspector visited all boats that plied up and down the canal and, if anyone were sick aboard, the boat was not allowed to stop within the boundaries of the city. The Common Council records refer the the appointment of Doctor Tonelier as City Physician at this time at $25.00 per annum; he was also allowed $7.25 for vaccinating the "yanses."

Dr. H.C. Van Zandt, the first Health Officer, was not appointed until 1882. In that same year, the first report of a Registrar of Vital Statistics was issued. Since reporting of births and deaths was not required, the registrar's records were not complete in these early years. Schenectady's public water supply, which was taken from the Mohawk River, was found to be contaminated in 1883. Accordingly a new water supply was developed from wells in Rotterdam in 1894. Also, in 1885 the City of Schenectady had the distinction of being the only city in the state where all dairies, which provided milk for city use, had been inspected for tuberculosis.

Epidemics were the chief cause of concern of the Board of Health at the turn of the century. The first contagious disease hospital, which was nothing more than a wooden barracks, was constructed on the present site of the City Hospital during the term of Dr. William Clute as Health Officer. Patients with various infectious diseases and conditions were mixed in together. It was Dr. Clute's practice to place a patient in a carriage for transportation to the hospital, and Dr. Clute would ride horseback ahead of the carriage ringing a bell in order to warn all persons to keep a good distance. It was at the end of Dr. Clute's term in 1907 that the Board of Health was abolished and its duties placed upon the Health Officer. During 1908, the Tuberculosis Dispensary was established and tuberculosis reporting was made compulsory; the dispensary was staffed by Doctors Gould, Pashayan, and McPartlon. Diphtheria antitoxin was first mentioned in 1910 and two successive negative cultures were required before the diphtheria patient could be released.

In 1913, a Baby Welfare Station opened for the purpose of dispensing milk to mothers and for the giving of advice regarding various problems of infancy and babyhood. The first Prenatal Clinic was established in 1916 with Doctor Wells in charge. Also, Well Child Clinics were opened in the public schools, where children were immunized against the various infectious diseases of childhood. During 1918, the great influenza pandemic hit Schenectady. There were 15,000 cases with 404 deaths. A Venereal Disease Clinic was opened in 1918 and remained in operation until its final demise in January 1960.

A Health Center was established in the old Mercy Hospital in the year 1919 and was moved in 1921 to 508 Union Street; in this center there were medical, surgical, gynecological, tuberculosis, nose and throat, and venereal disease clinics. This Health Center continued in operation until its closure in 1950, when clinics were opened in the hospitals of the County. A new, fireproof addition built to accommodate 60 patients was made to the City Hospital in 1925. Prior to 1926, public health nurses had been assigned to specific duties, such as tuberculosis nursing, maternal and child health nursing, etc. In that year, each nurse was assigned to a general program covering all the various home services and given a definite district of the city. In 1936, Dr. William Treder became the first full-time Health Officer in keeping with State legislation requiring that full-time Health Officers not practice medicine. The Schenectady Health Department assumed the administration of the Crippled Children's Program in 1949; under this program, persons under 21 years of age having crippling defects could have these defects corrected at State and County expense if their families were unable to pay for this care privately.

In 1946, State legislation required that all full-time Health Officers have a Master of Public Health degree in addition to their Doctor of Medicine. Also, in that year, 50% State financial aid became available for all approved public health programs. A Bureau of Environmental Sanitation was created in 1947 and Mr. Morris Mandel Cohn was appointed its head as Schenectady's first Sanitary Engineer. Also, the public health nursing service was completely re-organized and a Director, Miss Adrienne Proskine, appointed in 1949. The year 1954 was an outstanding year in preventive medicine as it was then that the Salk polio-myelitis vaccine was introduced and field trials of the vaccine were held in Schenectady County. Two new programs in the field of environmental sanitation were inaugurated between the years 1955 and 1960, namely, air pollution control and the control of ionizing radiation. Another program, and the latest one, is the adequate inspection and control of red meats, which are slaughtered locally. At the present time, the Schenectady Rehabilitation and Day Hospital, formerly the

City Hospital, is operating a "Day Hospital" as a pilot study with the New York State Department of Health in order to learn what type patients can be rehabilitated on an out-patient basis, thus reducing the costs and allowing the patient to remain at home with his family.

PROMINENT MEMBERS

Ellis Kellert, MD

In reviewing the minutes of our Society, including summaries of the scientific programs, Dr. Ellis Kellert stands out for his numerous contributions to our profession, our community and his colleagues.

This text appeared in his Death Resolution in 1968:

"... for many years an active, respected and beloved member of this Society... his opinion and wisdom were frequently sought after and were always freely available to his medical colleagues...he exercised a powerful influence on the elevation and improvement of medical practice and the advancement of medical science."

Dr. Arthur Penta described Dr. Kellert as a gentle and lovable man with a calm temperament, accurate and careful in observation, whose genuine friendliness gained him the respect of the entire community. He was foremost a teacher of his colleagues, and inculcated in them the highest conceptions of dignity of our profession.

Dr. Kellert was born in Albany in 1886 and graduated from Albany Medical College in 1909. He interned in Albany and completed his pathology training at what was then known as Harvard Cancer Hospital. There, he was associated with some of our nation's leading medical scientists including Cushing, Mallory, Councilman, and Smith, and others whose names we have read in our pathology textbooks. After service at the Yale Army Medical School during World War I, he directed Bender Laboratory and then came to Ellis in 1923, where he worked until his retirement in 1958.

His scientific contributions were impressive in number and importance. He published more than 30 papers in the fields of cancer, infectious diseases and the history of medicine. He wrote textbook chapters on psittacosis and infectious mononucleosis and described the first case of the latter diagnosis in Schenectady County. At the time of his final illness, he was writing a monograph on the history of the microscope in America. He was a member of numerous medical organizations, including Sigma Xi and Alpha Omega Alpha and he served as president of our Society.

The minutes of our scientific programs are replete with the presence of Dr. Kellert. He participated in discussions following hundreds of talks on all imaginable subjects for nearly 40 years. It is very easy to picture Dr. Kellert posing questions to out-of-town experts in order to clarify the relevance of the science to the care of patients at the bedside. He constantly encouraged his colleagues to remain true to the science of medicine and to increase their knowledge. (Note: The author met Dr. Kellert only once, at a Biology seminar at Union College. He was neatly dressed, short in stature and mild mannered. With a friendly smile on his face, he had a grandfatherly persona.)

Dr. Kellert served as the historian for our Society for many years and published several articles on the history of medicine in the Mohawk Valley. One such article about the Schenectady County Medical Society appeared in the *New York State Medical Journal* on our quasquicentennial.

At the annual meeting in June 1959, Dr. Kellert was honored on the 50th anniversary of his graduation from medical school. He commented on the *"...laudable conservatism of the medical profession and slowness of people in all walks of life in accepting the new in any field of endeavor, especially by those over forty years of age."*

Dr. Kellert noted that medical ethics were quite sound, standards were high and physicians were held in greater esteem than ever before, notwithstanding the outcry regarding the high cost of medical care at the time. He predicted a steady decline in practice by individual physicians and an increase in groups. He speculated about the advent of corporate practices emanating from hospitals, which increasingly became active community health centers with 'round-the-clock services.

He studied the origins of our insignia and, at the April 1962 meeting he requested help in identifying the physicians in the 1910 portrait. That year, he also created a display in the medical library, which included a combined lancet for venesection and scarifier for small pox vaccination, a hollow wooden stick stethoscope, and a gold-plated intubation set for treating laryngeal obstruction in diphtheria. Together with Prof. Leonard Clark, Dr. Kellert established the permanent exhibit of antique microscopes at Union College.

In 1969, Dr. Tischler presented a portrait of Dr. Kellert to the Medical Society. It was accepted by his successor as Chief of Pathology at Ellis, Dr. Parkhurst, who remembered Kellert as *"...quiet and unassuming but without peer in his field and will long be remembered by all of us who have been fortunate enough to have been associated with him."*

Ellis Kellert, MD

Daniel Toll, MD

Of the 41 physicians who formed the Medical Society of the County of Schenectady in 1810, we know the most about Daniel Toll. His formal portrait now hangs in the Society office. Dr. Toll appears to be in his mid-fifties at the time of the painting. His pudgy, clean-shaven face suggests his Dutch ancestry. He is not smiling, but his eyes reveal a touch of playfulness in an otherwise stern countenance. He is well dressed and holds a long-stemmed pipe with a curved clay bowl, of the type Rip Van Winkle might have used. And, the artist includes Dr. Toll's violin in the lower right-hand corner.

He was born in Schenectady in 1776 and, in all likelihood, his native tongue was Dutch. He was a contemporary of the eighth US president, Martin Van Buren, who was also of Dutch heritage and was born about 50 miles away, in Kinderhook, NY. Toll served a four-year apprenticeship with Dr. Alexander Adams, the first president of our Society. He received his license to practice in 1804, probably from a NYS Supreme Court Judge. The City Directory of 1841 lists Dr. Toll's office address as 10 Front St.

At our inaugural meeting in 1810, Dr. Toll was elected as our delegate to the State Society and to the first Board of Censors. The following year he was chosen to be our second President, a post he held until 1824, longer than anyone else in our history. He wrote the "Oath of Office" required for all candidates for membership in the early days (quoted in the Preface) and is responsible for the Grand Seal of our society.

During the smallpox epidemic of 1814, Dr. Toll, along with seven other physicians and Union College President Eliphalet Nott, signed a letter in the Schenectady Cabinet encouraging Schenectady residents to undergo vaccination. Dr. Toll came out of retirement in 1834 to treat victims of the Asian Cholera epidemic.

Dr. Toll was very active in civic affairs, especially in improving river navigation on the Mohawk River and, later, in the construction of the Erie Canal. He was also an author. In 1847, he published *"Early Dutch Settlers, with Anecdotal Eccentricities and Antiquities,"* in which he relates his genealogy and describes Dutch Architecture in early Schenectady. Insights into his character may be gleaned from the foreword of the book, written in his own legible handwriting. It is preserved in the collections of the Schenectady County Historical Society and, in it, he states:

"I have made neither show nor pretension nor neither have I exhibited any ostentation in the publication of my little work, but wonderful to relate having had almost half a century of intercourse with the men of letters, the men of science, and the men of religion including the faculty of Union College."

Our present Dr. Toll is actually "Richard the Third." Dr. Marselus Toll, who practiced in Scotia, was a direct descendent of Daniel Toll. Richard is not related.

Daniel Toll, MD

Janet Murray, MD

WOMEN JOIN OUR RANKS

Janet Murray, MD

The first woman to serve as a physician in Schenectady was Dr. Janet Murray. She was born in Scotland and moved to Canada at the age of 10. Her father was a minister and her mother was an invalid, for whom Janet was the caregiver. After she graduated from Women's Medical College of Kingston, Ontario 1891, she accepted an appointment as an intern in Boston, and had occasion to travel through Schenectady by train. For unknown reasons, her job in Boston was not to her liking, so she again boarded the train and got off at Schenectady because she liked the sound of the name as it was called out by the conductor. She was licensed to practice in 1891 by the New York State Board of Regents. When she began to practice at age 33, the population of Schenectady was 20,000. Her first office was located above a tailor's shop on Jay Street.

In 1897, Dr. Murray was elected Vice-President of the Society. She was nominated from the floor on the fifth ballot, after candidates on the first four ballots failed to achieve a majority. The following year, she was nominated for president and received only one vote. However, she was evidently a good sport because she hosted the entire Society at her home for the April 1902 meeting.

It is likely that Dr. Murray included obstetrics in her practice because at the December 1904 meeting she presented a scientific paper entitled *"A Case of Lacerated Perineum where the Head came into the Rectum."* In 1915, the Ellis Hospital School of Nursing engaged Dr. Murray to lecture on the subject of eugenics and hygiene. She served as attending physician at the Old Ladies Home for over forty years.

During a newspaper interview marking her 42nd year of practice, she said *"tell them that 42 years is not so far away after all...the baggage car ambulances don't seem so far away."* (Perhaps she was referring to the transport of sick and injured patients to the hospital by railroad baggage car, since she began her practice before motorized ambulances.) Before the interview concluded, she abruptly dismissed the reporter so she could make a house call.

Dr. Murray practiced in Schenectady for 46 years. She was a member of the First Presbyterian Church and an Honorary Member of the Schenectady Business and Professional Women's Club, as well as the Women's Medical Society, MSSNY and the AMA. When she died in February 1940 at age 83, our Society placed a "Resolution of Respect" in a local newspaper. This article cited her *"dignity, personal charm, cheerfulness, devotion to work, and exceptional ability to work with others."*

Elizabeth Gillette, MD

Elizabeth Van Rensselaer Gillette, MD

Elizabeth Gillette, the second woman to join our Society, had a fascinating life even before coming to Schenectady. She was a native of Granby, Connecticut, and graduated from New York Medical College and Hospital for Women in 1898. She moved here in 1900 and opened her office on June 1. Much to her surprise, she was visited by many local physicians, including Dr. Kathan, who made her feel welcome in Schenectady and she was invited to join our Society in 1904.

Early on, she was asked to make a house call for Mrs. Welton Stanford who lived in the mansion at the corner of State Street and Balltown Road. This building later became the Ingersoll Home, and the neighborhood is known as Stanford Heights. In 1900, the Schenectady horse-pulled trolley only traveled State Street as far as Fehr Avenue, so Dr. Gillette had to walk the rest of the way (about 2 miles). As her practice grew, she was able to afford her own horse-and-buggy and, in 1904, she purchased her first car—a two-cylinder, 14-horsepower Maxwell. She was one of the first women in Schenectady to drive. No license plates or insurance were needed.

When the Workmen's Compensation law was enacted, General Electric gave her office space at their plant and, with the help of a nurse, she saw up to "30 girls a day." In addition, she performed pre-employment physicals on about 400 workers. When her own practice became too busy, she had to leave GE.

Aside from being a dedicated physician, she was an active member of the community. After she witnessing much cruelty to the children of poor families in her practice, she founded the Humane Society. She recruited President Raymond of Union College to her support cause, and the city fathers were invited to the first meeting at the President's House, on campus. For years, subsequent meetings were held in Dr. Gillette's office, she served for a long time as treasurer of the organization, and it later led to the establishment of the Schenectady Childrens' Home.

In 1919, Dr. Gillette was the first Upstate assemblywoman elected in NYS. The Nineteenth Amendment to the Constitution, Women's Suffrage, was not in effect until the following year. Remarkably, she won without the women' vote. She was also the first Democrat to represent the district in 30 years. Dr. Gillette advocated for legislation to improve the public health, including the examination of all children employed in factories by the State Industrial Commission and the requirement that certain medications be certified by the Farm and Markets Department. She served on the Banking and Education Committees, and voted to legalize boxing in New York State.

Dr. Gillette had this advice for women wishing to seek public office: *"Vote in every election, go to every political meeting possible, learn all you can about political affairs — and always be a lady."*

In a 1955 newspaper interview, she described herself as *"one of those hard core stubborn Connecticut Yankees."* By then, she was no longer making house calls or delivering babies. She added, *"I'm not in the operating room any more but I still set broken bones, something I love to do. I will continue as long as my body will let me, I want to die in harness."*

Dr. Gillette practiced until 1959 and died in 1965 at age 90. Her death resolution described her as *"a rugged individualist, tenacious in purpose and voicing her opinions on community matters in vigorous fashion so characteristic of her. Her passing is a matter of deep regret to the community she served so long and so well."*

Interestingly, Dr. Gillette's name does not appear in listings of the medical staff at Ellis Hospital, even though she was a surgeon with a special interest in diseases of the sinuses. In those days, patients often underwent surgery on their kitchen tables. Perhaps she performed her surgery at the hospital at 404 Union Street, which was known at different times as Mercy Hospital, Physicians Hospital, and Sisters Hospital. The hospital first opened in 1907 and contained 30 beds and an operating room. It closed in 1917, but was reopened as Emergency Hospital for a few months in the autumn of 1918 during the Spanish Flu epidemic.

Dr. Murray is the only woman among the 28 physicians who appear in the 1894 composite. By 1910, there were 6 women and 80 men. In 1926, however, Dr. Murray and Dr. Gillette are the only two women among of 116 members. It is uncertain what became of the other 4 women.

A Bit of Trivia

At our February 1980 meeting, Dr. Helen Keigher became the only member in the history of our Society to be elected as a member three different times! She first joined us in 1945 as a general practitioner when she joined her father's practice. In 1952, she resigned to raise her five children. She then completed a pathology residency and joined us for the second time in 1963. She resigned once again in 1977, only to return for a third time in 1980 as Associate Pathologist at Ellis Hospital.

POTPOURRI

The following excerpts, drawn from our minutes, recount less momentous but nonetheless interesting, amusing and/or unique occurrences in our past.

June 1892: The Presidential Address was *"Reminiscences of Earlier Practitioners"* and the Historian spoke on the personal histories of members prior to the Society's reorganization. (Oh to have witnessed this!)

June 1896: Dr. H. read a very interesting paper on a case of extremely aggravated prolapse of the uterus complicated by pregnancy. Dr. Mynderse gave the members a very scrumptious repast of all the dainties of the season after which the members enjoyed a smoke upon the broad piazzas of the doctor's residence. A shower accompanied by a loud thunderclap followed by a most beautiful rainbow was the feature of the afternoon.

May 1903: Dr. Clowe reported on his trip to Africa, and Dr. Hughes on his trip to South America.

June 1908: At a meeting held at Saratoga Lake, the Society advocated for a psychopathic ward where patients might go voluntarily or be taken in insane for observation.

May 1926: The fee for a lunacy examination from the County was $5.00, whereas the neighboring county pays their physicians $10.00 for a lunacy exam.

May 1935: Dr. Blake spoke on the wines of France. The talk was not only interesting, but spiritual. The discourse was illustrated by very good samples of the wines of France.

December 1942: Health Commissioner, Dr. Treder, asked Society members to carefully examine the legs and clothing of any patient who complained of bites on the leg after attending a local theater, which was reported to be infested. (The identity of the theater was kept confidential by the Society - for obvious reasons!)

December 1944: Dr. Clowe reported on the penicillin situation: use cautiously so we don't overdraw our quota.

December 1947: Dr. Clowe read a letter from an individual who was injured while attending a dance and was treated by a local physician. Since she didn't have $5.00 to pay his fee, he requested and accepted her friend's watch as security.

January 1952: At a lecture on pneumonia by Dr. Russell Cecil, Professor of Medicine at Columbia University, Dr. Clowe asked, *"What should I do if the patient wants antibiotics and I don't think she has a bacterial pneumonia?"* Some things haven't changed in 58 years.

March 1952: Miss McConnell, Superintendent at Sunnyview, asked the doctors not to park on the hospital lawn when attending meetings, and also to please use the ashtrays when smoking to avoid damage to the flooring.

November 1952: A meeting will be held with the editors of both Schenectady newspapers to improve relations with the press.

November 1953: It was suggested to the incoming entertainment committee that less spiritus fermenti be served. (See next item.)

November 1953: The Society was asked to submit the names of 6 physicians to the County Board of Supervisors, who will choose one to serve on the Division of Alcohol. (See previous item.)

November 1956: A congratulatory telegram was sent to Oswald D. Heck as our Assembly Representative for 26 years and Leader for 20 years. (A residential facility for disabled persons was subsequently built on Balltown Road and named for him.)

February 1957: Dr. Clowe announced that the date of the dinner-dance of the Women's Auxiliary was changed, because no orchestra was available. Tickets can be purchased from Dr. Holmblad.

January 1957: The Society defeated a motion to approve WRGB showing an American Cancer Society film on *"Self-Examination of the Breast"* on television. (This was after viewing the film during the annual meeting at the Van Curler Hotel). The following month, the film was approved to be shown in a local theater to a female-only audience.

December 1961: The Sick Committee reported that its expenses of $104.45 for flowers and fruit baskets were the lowest in 10 years due to the excellent health of our members.

December 1961: Censors are investigating allegations that certain members are "charging exorbitant fees."

December 1961: A motion was approved to increase the salary of Mrs. Smith, our administrative secretary, by 10% to show our appreciation for her excellent performance. Three years later, the Society voted to pay for her parking permit.

October 1962: Dr. Horowitz, Chair of the Hospital and Professional Relations Committee, concluded that with *"individual physicians aiding and abetting the use of the Emergency Room, nothing could be done to halt the practice of medicine by the hospital."*

November 1963: GE presented an open house for physicians on use of computers in managing accounts receivable and other business functions.

December 1963: Our President announced that the Chairman of the Sick Committee was in the hospital. Our Secretary was instructed, with unanimous approval of the members, to write a letter to the Chairman expressing the Society's concern and good wishes.

December 1963: Dr. Ritterband was granted permission to address the members on an issue with political overtones.

February 1964: Dr. Clowe was chosen to serve as a judge for the Schenectady Junior Miss Pageant.

February 1964: Dr. Hans Rozendaal reported on his second transatlantic crossing on his 38-foot yacht. Dr. Byrne Mayer accompanied him on his first crossing.

March 1965: Dr. Blake was elected President of MSSNY.

May 1965: The Schenectady County Pharmaceutical Society requested that we sign prescriptions legibly, and not ask any pharmacist to dispense a narcotic without a written prescription in hand. *"The law does not care about our problems or patients' suffering,"* they noted.

March 1966: The Schenectady Union Star newspaper inquired what the Medical Society was doing about teenage drug addiction. At the April meeting, Dr. Joseph DeBlase stated there was no known problem with teenage addiction in this area.

April 1966: The Society opposed the use of Schenectady General Depot as a Chiropractic College and advocated for its use as a community college.

April 1967: The Society members agreed to provide their favorite recipes in their own handwriting for a cookbook created by the Auxiliary to raise money for nursing scholarships.

October 1967: Dr. George Graham was elected President of the American Hospital Association.

May 1968: Dr. Clowe offered his talents in directing and producing "Up, Up and Away" with the Ellis Nursing students and the Doctors' Orchestra at Linton High School.

May 1968: Dr. Jameson, Dr. Marsh, Dr. Voss, Dr. Van Ness, and Dr. Geller were called to military duty during the Vietnam war.

December 1969: Dr. Pulver reported on a maternal death due to sepsis resulting from an illegal abortion, and stated that the woman's life probably could have been saved if her procedure had been performed in competent, professional hands in a modern hospital.

March 1970: Dr. Brown moved that the Society endorse repeal and reform of the [then-current] abortion law. Dr. Sullivan dissented, stating than many members' personal opinions did not support repeal. The motion passed, but not unanimously.

February 1971: St. Faith's House in Tarrytown, NY acquainted us with services for unmarried pregnant girls.

February 1972: The Federal government enacted a rule requiring physicians to post notices in their offices that a fee schedule is available for any patient's perusal, and offices would be subject to inspections for compliance. In addition, we were allowed to raise our fees by only 2.5 %.

October 1975: A complaint was received from Dr. Arony about the excessive noise and speed of ambulances.

May 1979: Dr. Giknis objected to placing patients' beds in hospital hallways, claiming that it is dehumanizing and undignified. (This was done mostly at Ellis during the nursing home bed crisis; see below.)

April 1980: A letter was received from the Health Services in Correctional Institutions Committee of MSSNY commending Dr. James Purcell for providing quality health care at the County jail.

June 1980: Dr. Mason, Dr. Holmblad and Dr. Drago gave reports on the services they provided at the 1980 Winter Olympics in Lake Placid.

December 1980: Dr. Breault reported that there are now 114 active malpractice cases, some of which involve several physicians. Many of the Society's deliberations were (and continue to be) about malpractice insurance.

January 1981: Dr. Warner, age 101, called the Society from the Teresian House to thank us for his Christmas gift. An otolaryngologist, Warner was a founder of Sunnyview Hospital.

He graduated Lansingburgh High School in Troy and entered Albany Medical College, graduating in 1906. He was a member of Kiwanis for 78 years.

January 1981: Dr. Sulllivan explained that Hospice is an organization that provides care for terminally ill patients and it needs our emotional and financial support.

June 1982: Doc Spring's Rehabilitated Dixieland Band provided the entertainment for our Annual Meeting. In addition to Dr. Spring on the trumpet, there were Dr. Joe Slovak on clarinet, Dr. Sam Strauss on saxophone, and Dr. Jim Strosberg on tuba. Later, Dr. John Angerosa (formerly a star on WRGB Teenage Barn) joined the band on the piano.

January 1983: Health Commissioner David Axelrod notified physicians that treatment of patients in facilities unlicensed by the State is professional misconduct and could jeopardize their license to practice medicine.

February 1983: Dr. Tytko thanked us for the poinsettia plant that the Society sent to him for the holidays.

June 1984: Dr. Fulco, Dr. Panneton, and Judge Robert Lynch organized the first inter-professional dinner with the Bar Association and Dental Society. Annual meetings featuring invited speakers have been held for more than 25 years.

April 1985: Our Society hired a bus to bring members to a malpractice reform rally at the State Capitol in Albany.

May 1989: Dr. Lange reported that MSSNY passed a resolution (by a vote of 300 to 5) calling for removal of Dr. Axelrod as Commissioner of Health. (However, Governor Cuomo did not take our advice.)

January 1990: Dr. Lange spoke about living wills, and made a motion to have the Medical Society print samples for primary care offices.

July 1992: A congratulatory telegram was sent to Dr. John Clowe on his inauguration as President of the AMA.

January 1995: Dr. Robert Kennedy made a motion encouraging MVP to build its new office building in Schenectady.

April 1999: The Society passed Dr. Tepper's resolution that smoking should be banned in all restaurants in Schenectady.

May 1999: The Comitia Minora passed Dr. McEvoy's resolution that MVP headquarters remain in Schenectady.

FEES AND COLLECTIONS

During the 19th century, there were numerous entries in the minutes concerning fees. As early as 1871, the Society discussed chronic impecuniosity. The policy endorsed in September 1897 called for *"...a minimum and a maximum for every operation, the former should be stationary and the latter elastic subject to the discretion of the physician."* (Soak the rich, and don't give the poor a break?) This might have been the official policy, but it's hard to believe this was actually observed by our medical predecessors. Those of us who had fathers and grandfathers in practice in the days before Medicaid are familiar with the amount of uncompensated care they provided to the poor.

In January 1903, the Society increased the fee for house calls from $1.50 to $2.00 and, during the April meeting, raised the fees for difficult obstetrical confinements from $25 to $100, for hip fractures from $50 to $120, for dilatation and curettage (D&C) from $10 to $50, and for foreign body in the eye from $2 to $25.

In 1889, in an attempt to protect our economic interests, the Society published a "deadbeat" list. These were patients who did not pay their doctor. When a physician's good will was exhausted, the patient would just find another one. This initiative was carried out by the *Protective Association of the Physicians of Schenectady*, probably just a name change to enable the Society to avoid liability. A 24-page booklet was printed by *The Schenectady Gazette*, and the 27 names listed inside the front cover comprised all of the practicing physicians in Schenectady. The names of 630 "deadbeats" appeared in alphabetical order, alongside the initials of the reporting physicians.

The cover of the booklet was imprinted with the words: *"Confidential to All Members."* The booklet began with the following disclaimer: *"Members will observe that this publication is strictly confidential to them...it is not to be shown to any other person. This record is not intended to express any judgement on the honesty or dishonesty, solvency or insolvency of any person whatsoever."* This 120-year-old booklet is in excellent condition and is kept at the Efner Historical Center in City Hall for those wishing to know if their ancestors appear in the list of deadbeats. Check it out!

After reading our minutes from the past two centuries, it is hard to escape the conclusion that—while many physicians are politically conservative—most are very charitable when it comes to patient care. This history presents numerous examples of collective and personal charity, including the free care and cash donations provided to support the Schenectady Free Clinic today.

SMIT COMMITTEE

Schenectady County has recently endured the upheaval caused by the closure of St. Clare's and Bellevue Hospitals and the need for Ellis to assume their operating licenses. The NYS Commission on Health Care Facilities in the 21st Century (a/k/a Berger Commission) was charged with eliminating waste, duplication of services and money-losing hospitals throughout the state. The axe fell heavily on Schenectady. Perhaps, if our hospital Boards and Administrators had followed our Society's advice, the outcome might have been different.

At the November 1995 meeting, Dr. Robert Kennedy commented on health care in the community and and the possibility of a joint venture between the two major hospitals to control costs down and improve the quality of care. He urged the physicians of the community to be leaders in this effort. At that time, there was a small health coordination subcommittee consisting of Drs. John Kennedy, Purcell, Routenberg and Skudder. President Strosberg expanded this committee and appointed Dr. Gary Wood as Chairman. The original name of this committee was the Schenectady Health Integration Task Force, but this was soon changed to the Schenectady Medical Integration Task Force so the acronym could be used.

Dr. Wood provided outstanding leadership. Meetings were held alternately at Ellis and St. Clare's Hospitals. At least half of the committee members were primary care physicians. Its mission was to effect integration of care in Schenectady, in view of estimates from the Hospital Association of New York State (HANYS) that Federal health care funding for NYS would decrease by $100 million over the ensuing seven years. The committee's report noted *"excellent providers in community, but [they] function in variable degrees of cooperation, often with duplication of services and over-utilization."*

The SMIT committee met numerous times over several years. Discussions included leaders of MVP Healthcare and GE Power Systems, and senior administrators at both hospitals. Sadly, the hospitals were not willing to engage in formal, comprehensive planning to restructure services in a consolidated fashion. They could not even agree to maintain a common patient database. At most, they were willing to consider rationalization of specific, selected services.

At the June 1996 meeting, on an original motion by Dr. Sattar amended by Dr. Jakubowski, the Society voted almost unanimously that *"Ellis and St Clare's combine obstetrics and pediatrics in a manner to be determined by the medical staffs and hospitals, and hospitals formalize an arrangement for specialty and tertiary care referrals."*

The original intent was for St. Clare's to provide provide all obstetrical and pediatric care, and for Ellis to provide tertiary and subspecialty care. If the hospitals had only heeded the advice of SMIT, they might not have been smitten by Berger.

IN THE PAST

Compiled By James M. Strosberg, MD

Based upon documents and interviews by Roy Keigher, MD, with Edward Wienecke, MD

Dr Roy Keigher was a past-president who served as Historian for many years. His original manuscripts are preserved at the Efner Historical Center in City Hall. Among them is an unpublished interview he conducted in October 1949. Here are excerpts from this unedited interview entitled "A Talk with Dr. Edward Wienecke, 28 Jay St."

"Dr. Edward Wienecke is one of the older Physicians of Schenectady, in fact today the oldest member of the Schenectady County Medical Society; he is 75 yrs. old; he was born and educated in Schenectady, he is a graduate of Albany Medical College. He is about the last contact we have with those who, when Dr. Wienecke was a young man, were old between 1885 and 1900. Today he was in bed recovering from a colostomy performed by Dr. E. MacDonald Stanton for carcinoma of the sigmoid at the Ellis Hospital. He was cheerful and very clear mentally, remembering details about the older M.D.s. The following are some of the Physicians he talked about:

"Dr. I. Piffier - a charleton [sic], faker; he lived next door to Dr. Wienecke on 506 State St. when Dr. Wienecke started in practice. Dr. Wienecke said that Piffier cured by laying on the hands and the people flocked to him, including some of the best people in Schenectady; Dr. Wienecke envied him in view of the fact that he did not have any practice at that time. The County Medical Society finally got fed up on Piffier and had him run out of town.

"Dr. Markey - a graduate of Albany Medical College about 1893; he lived at one time on Broadway, he was student of Dr. Schoolcraft; he became a very heavy drinker and dope fiend and died as a comparatively young man; he was indicted by a grand jury at one time for doing an abortion but was never convicted. He was a brother of Mrs. Frank DeForest who is the wife of the plumber and is still alive; Markey's father worked in the American Locomotive Works (Big Shop), quit and opened a saloon near the ALCO. Many of the workmen would go over to his saloon and get half stewed and be incapable of work the rest of the day. ALCO offered Markey a job back but he refused; Dr. Markey married a daughter of Mike Barrett; rumor had it that Dr. Markey committed suicide when he died.

"Dr. D. E. Spoor - father of Dr. Walter Spoor, born in Denver, Col; a homopath [sic]; had an office on Lafayette St; while driving car up Furman St. hill, brakes did not hold, car backed down hill out of control and Dr Spoor (Sr.) was killed; he was not a member of the Schenectady County Medical Society.

"Dr. Walter Spoor - son of Dr. D.E. Spoor; a homopath [sic], did a lot of physiotherapy, electric; had a colostomy at Ellis for cancer of the large gut and subsequently died, not a member of the Schenectady County Medical Society.

"Dr. A.J. Young - Mrs. Wienecke said she remembered Dr. Young when he would come into the old Mercy Hospital; he would leave a number of kinds of medicine and ask the nurses if they were good for the patient.

"Dr. Hammer - born in Germany; not a graduate of any medical college; licensed by the State of New York; Dr. Hammer wore a beard, was very neat about his clothes; had bunions; was attending physician to the old Ellis family and lived at one time in the old Ellis home at corner of Liberty and Erie Blvd.; Dr. Hammer was on staff of the old Ellis Hos. on Jay St; spoke English with a German accent. Dr. Hammer attended my mother (Mary Keigher) when I was born on lower State Street in 1885.

"Dr. James Barry - had an office on Union St., never married. Dr. Wienecke said he called in Dr. Barry in consultation to see a case of erysipelas and Dr. Barry died a few days after of Bright's Disease. He was between 35 and 40 years of age; he has a brother still alive who fits eyeglasses.

"Dr. Wienecke told me about a meeting of the Medical Society out to Dr. Ennis's home in Pattersonville; I do not know the exact date but it must have been about 1895. The Society had chartered the old Kitty West and all were waiting for Dr. Abraham Jacobi from New York to arrive; he was the speaker for the day. Drs. Wienecke and McMullen were appointed a committee of two to escort Dr. Jacobi to the Kitty West. They went over to the Railroad Station and spotted Dr. Jacobi; they had been given a description of him beforehand. He was a short man with a large shock of hair giving him a leonine look; he always wore a cape. Wienecke and McMullen took him over to the Kitty West, which was in the old Erie Canal a very short distance from the Railroad Station. All members of the Society with whom I have talked with [sic] about the treatment accorded Dr. Jacobi agree that it was terrible; the members paid no attention to him except Wienecke and McMullen; the members played poker and shot crap on the deck of the Kitty West on the trip to Pattersonville and after the meeting Dr. Jacobi was allowed to shift for himself. He remarked about the treatment accorded him but after he did write both Wienecke and McMullen thanking them for looking after him. Dr. Jacobi was at that time one of the outstanding physicians of New York City; He did a lot of pediatrics and was thought a specialist in this line. He was of Jewish extraction; he married a woman physician, but I am told that their marriage went of [sic] the rocks. He usually took one teaspoonful of brandy before retiring. He had a summer home on Lake George and died in the fire when this camp burned."

*   *   *

Dr. Jacobi was, indeed, a pioneer in pediatrics. He opened the first pediatric clinic in the United States, and served as President of MSSNY and of the AMA. He was a founder of the American Journal of Obstetrics. At the time of his visit to our Society and his voyage on the old Kitty West, he was on the faculty of Columbia University. What a shame on our society for our treatment of such a prominent guest! However, Dr. Jacobi apparently did not hold a grudge. In 1910, he was a featured speaker at our Centennial Celebration, and his talk was entitled "The Educational Value of the County Medical Society."

*   *   *

THE FOLLOWING IS A TRANSCRIPT OF
A GYNECOLOGY CONSULTATION CIRCA 1950

(Letter sent to Dr. Reynolds from an Albany Obstetrician/Gynecologist)

"I saw Mrs. Blank today. She says she feels lots better than she has been feeling. Of course I don't know how badly she has been feeling but I do know she has had an unusually slow, tedious convalescence but nothing we can put our finger on, but I have a feeling that she wasn't too good before we operated on her. We like to blame something besides ourselves.

"I don't know just how to acount [sic] for it. Anyway she says she has gained weight and feels lots better and she looks better. The vault of the vagina is a little slow in healing. I don't think it necessarily means anything. And the cuff on the right side feels slightly indurated. It isn't anything I can put my hand on but I am sure eventually it will straighten itself out. I encouraged her to get outdoors and do things. I think she can regain her strenght [sic] only by using the strenght [sic] she has. I do think iron and a tonic will help her. More power to her. To you too. Hope the blue thistle will be pretty this summer."

SECTION 2

From Individual Contributors

ELLIS HOSPITAL

By Michael Jakubowski, MD

In the last half of the 19th century, Schenectady was a major hub of industry and transportation for the northeastern United States. In 1883, the Schenectady Evening Star published an editorial on the lack of care for men involved in industrial accidents. It was necessary for injured workers to be transported to Albany, which was a long journey in those days. That editorial was the first public agitation for a hospital in Schenectady.

As a result, the Schenectady Free Dispensary opened in 1885. It was a facility with a five-bed ward clinical that enabled care of patients in Schenectady and eliminated the need for transport. The first patient admitted to the dispensary was John Snyder, a 37-year-old newspaperman. He had typhoid fever, from which he recovered and was discharged one month later. Only 8 of the first 24 patients admitted were native-born, reflecting the sizable immigration into Schenectady during the 1890s.

In 1891, Charles G. Ellis died. He had been President of Schenectady Locomotive Works, and left a bequest of $25,000 toward the construction of a hospital to be called Ellis Hospital. Two years later, the Schenectady Free Dispensary was dissolved and Ellis Hospital, a 30-bed facility, opened on Jay Street. The medical staff that first year included Drs. Robert Fuller and William L. Pearson as consulting physicians and surgeons. Drs. George E. McDonald, Charles C. Duryee, John L. Schoolcraft, Charles Hammer, Henry Van Zandt and John A. Heatley were members of the house staff.

In the same year, without government mandate, Hospital President, Alonzo P. Strong, proclaimed "A patient's admission is in no sense dependent upon his ability to pay. Anyone who is unable to pay receives the same attention as a paying patient."

A training school for nurses was established at Ellis in 1903 by Miss Ella Underhill, and a permanent nurse training charter was granted by NYS in 1917. The Hospital Association purchased six acres of land off Nott Street for a new and larger hospital, using a bequest from Dr. Fuller. In 1906, Ellis Hospital moved to its present Nott Street location. The Whitmore Home, a residence for student nurses, was constructed nearby and the hospital pharmacy was established.

In 1908, construction of C wing gave the hospital a total of 100 beds. The Locomotive works presented an ALCO automobile ambulance to the hospital in 1911. The first community-wide hospital fund drive was held in 1914, and raised $106,000 for hospital expansion. This enabled opening of the A Wing, with three floors providing 75 beds and an open-air sun porch. A Pathological Laboratory was also established.

In 1918, the hospital and its staff battled the outbreak of Spanish Influenza. Approximately 15,000 persons in Schenectady County were stricken with the flu, but only 404 died. The doctors and nurses of Ellis Hospital worked day and night to care for patients. There were 105 physicians in Schenectady in 1918, when the Hospital was accredited for its excellence by the American College of Surgeons.

During the 1920s, a major fund-raising drive, *"Help Your Hospital,"* netted $436,000 in public subscriptions. This enabled installation of high-pressure boilers, construction of the E Wing, and addition of a fourth floor to the A Wing for a children's ward. An Ellis Hospital Technology School was also established.

Toward the end of the decade, D Wing opened with 100 additional beds, for a total of 275; an extensive addition to Whitmore Home was completed, providing classrooms and more housing for student nurses. Another floor was added to C Wing to house six modern, completely equipped operating rooms.

During the 1930s, a women's volunteer organization, Pink Ladies, was founded and a Junior Aide program was also established. Another building drive raised $852,000, exceeding its goal of $700,000. B-Wing was completed with these funds, adding 139 beds and 49 bassinets.

Ellis Hospital became affiliated with the Albany Medical College in 1943, and in 1946 the Council on Medical Education of the AMA approved residency training programs in Medicine and Surgery. Subsequently, approval was granted for training programs in other fields. In 1949, Gov. Thomas E. Dewey selected Ellis Hospital as one of two hospitals in NYS to conduct an experimental program in psychiatric treatment.

In 1952, the hospital instituted a program of educational opportunities for the nursing and medical-dental staffs. The Schenectady County Heart Committee donated a ballistocardiograph, which enabled physicians to measure the mechanical movement of the heart and detect heart disease earlier than previously possible. A radiographic and fluoroscopic X-ray table was installed and in 1958, along with an X-Omat, which developed and dried X-ray film in six minutes. Existing methods required an hour or more.

During the 1950s, community support for the Hospital remained strong. A fund-raising drive in 1956 for renovation of the B wing raised $3,075,000 against a goal of $2,000,000. The B

Wing was enlarged by expansion and addition of two more floors. In another cardiology milestone, the first cardiac monitor pacemakers used at Ellis were inserted 1959.

The 1960s witnessed the addition of several new programs. A psychiatric day hospital was established to provide a therapeutic environment for psychiatric patients needing treatment but not full-time hospitalization. A Teletrol system was installed in the Radiology Department to help power new and more sophisticated equipment. Construction on H-Wing was completed, providing an expanded Emergency Room and 132 additional beds on four floors. The D-4 unit was opened for care of neurological and neurosurgical patients, and a new Coronary Care Unit opened. In 1969, the Kidney Disease Institute of the NYS DOH designated Ellis Hospital as a satellite treatment center for patients with chronic kidney disease.

Two years later, in 1971, the leaders of Ellis and Sunnyview cooperated in the construction of a new heating plant that would serve both hospitals. A year later, two additional floors were added to the H wing, with a surgical unit on H-5 and the Intensive Care Unit on H-6. Ultrasound equipment was added to the Radiology Department's diagnostic services. Physical therapy outpatient services were reactivated.

In 1975, the E Wing was demolished and construction began on the Clinical Services Building. When this was completed in 1977, the new Emergency Department opened. At this time, Ellis was serving as the Capital Region's major Trauma Center and, within 2 years, began an emergency airlift program in cooperation with the NY State Police helicopter unit, using the field behind the WGY-WRGB studios on Balltown Road as a helipad.

At around the same time, Ellis installed the first computerized tomography (CT) head scanner in Schenectady County, and the Internal Medicine Ambulatory Center (IMAC) clinic began providing ambulatory care services to the community. A fifty-bed Critical Care Center was established under the leadership of Drs. Karl Adler and Eric Rackow, Chief of Medicine and Director of Critical Care Services, respectively. Ellis had become a major center for cancer treatment and purchased a Linear Accelerator, the most advanced equipment available for radiation therapy at that time.

In the early 1980s, Ellis entered into a contractual arrangement with the Hospital Corporation of America (HCA) to provide management services, in what later proved to be a controversial and somewhat unpopular decision. The Ellis Hospital Foundation was founded to encourage corporate giving, to solidify charitable support from the community and to provide better coordination of gifts to the hospital.

Ellis established a Chronic Disease Care Program established to improve the quality of care and services for non-institutionalized individuals with chronic illnesses. A Pediatric Intensive

Care Unit was opened to enable physicians in Schenectady to care for more seriously ill children without transferring them to Albany.

The Nuclear Medicine Department installed a large-field gamma camera to enable more effective diagnoses of malignancies, bone disorders and blood clots. Radiology acquired Digital Subtraction Angiography (DSA) for the diagnosis of circulatory problems, and a full-body CT scanner was installed. A new Cardiac Rehabilitation program offered a graduated series of exercises for patients recovering from heart attacks or other cardiac conditions. The Neurology Department installed Real-Time Small-Part Ultrasound for measuring blood flow to the brain and, in Ophthalmology, an argon laser and a diagnostic ultrasound unit were used for better diagnosis and treatment of eye problems. And, in another major development, the Cardiac Catheterization Laboratory opened in 1984 with computerized equipment capable of pinpointing the source of heart problems.

In 1985, the Hospital celebrated its Centennial activities with publication of a hospital calendar and a centennial history book, "Hospital on the Hill," by local historian, Larry Hart. Ellis sponsored various exhibits, and created a time capsule to be incorporated into future construction. Toward the end of the decade, a new information management system was installed, with improved capabilities for storing and retrieving demographic and clinical data.

Excellence in the diagnosis and treatment of cardiac diseases continued and the first open heart surgery at Ellis Hospital was performed in 1991. In the 1990s, the Capital District Skins Game made its debut as a fund-raiser for the hospital's clinical services. This popular event has drawn professional golfers to the area each year and has been a major source of revenue for improving facilities and programs. In 1991, Ellis took a major step in adding cardiac surgery to its existing Cardiology services. Nearly 20 years later, Ellis continues to be a Center of Excellence for the diagnosis and treatment of heart disease.

During the same decade, it became apparent that a larger portion of healthcare services was being performed in the outpatient setting. In response to this, Ellis opened The Bruggeman Center for Diagnosis & Treatment, a state-of-the-art ambulatory care facility named in honor of Warren and Pauline Bruggeman for their generous support of the hospital.

With the turn of the 21st century, Ellis received a $100,000 grant from NYS to purchase the equipment needed to perform Radioactive Seed Implantation Therapy Program for prostate cancer. The Hospital's mammography unit was renamed the Mary J. Kakretz Mammography Unit, in memory of Ms. Kakretz for her philanthropy, and digital mammography equipment was installed.

The hospital earned national recognition by being named to the list of *"Top 100 Hospitals"* for its Heart Center its Intensive Care Unit. Ellis also became one of two hospitals to receive the inaugural NYS DOH Hospital Patient Safety Award for its success in reducing the incidence of Deep Vein Thrombosis (potentially deadly blood clots) in hospitalized patients.

The Foundation launched a $16-million capital campaign called *"The Campaign for Ellis Hospital: The Heart of Health Care in Our Community."* The Foundation received its largest contribution ever—a $2 million anonymous gift to support programs and services at the hospital.

Technology continued to advance with purchase of a new CT scanner, and construction of a new angiography suite with 3-dimensional rotational angiography. A new linear accelerator with intensity-modulated radiation therapy (IMRT) capabilities was added to the Radiation Oncology Department.

In 2004 Ellis Hospital became one of only three hospitals in the state to earn accreditation as a primary stroke center by the Joint Commission on Accreditation of Healthcare Organizations. The School of Nursing expanded to new Belanger Campus on Erie Boulevard in order to accommodate increased enrollment.

A new, two-story, 36-bed Intensive Care Unit opened, and was named for Ms. Beulah T. Hinkle, a major benefactor. This facility ushered in a new era of sophistication in Critical Care Medicine. Ellis became the only hospital in NYS to rank among the top 5% of hospitals nationwide for clinical excellence and patient safety in 2007, according to Health Grades, a leading national healthcare ratings organization.

As significant as these accomplishments were, the first decade of the 21st century will likely be remembered most by the activity of the Berger Commission. As noted above, the Commssion's report—released in November 2006—mandated that St. Clare's Hospital and Bellevue Woman's Hospital surrender their operating licenses to the DOH. In turn, Ellis Hospital assumed responsibility for all operations and services previously provided at St. Clare's and Bellevue. For the first time since the 19th century, Schenectady became a "one-hospital city."

Ellis Hospital, historical photograph

ST. CLARE'S HOSPITAL

Adapted from the website: www.rememberstclares.org

By Michael Jakubowski, MD

The St. Clare's story is one worth telling. Though not a very long story—barely 60 years from beginning to end—it is filled with passion and pride and a healing spirit that exemplifies the best in health care.

Its history is easily divided among two generations. The first gave rise to the hospital in the 1940s, helping to fund it, build it and sustain it over the course of their lives. The second generation inherited that mantle and kept the spirit alive even as the final chapter was being written.

St. Clare's Hospital did not just happen. Men and women of every creed and race, and from all economic and social strata, gave their time and effort—and their savings—to make possible the construction of this hospital. The story of St. Clare's goes back 93 years, to 1917, when Bishop Thomas Cusack purchased a piece of property on Bradley Street. A small section of this property is now used for parking and a bit more for an exit to Bradley Street.

Twenty years later, the Bishop of Albany, Edmund Gibbons said that that he would relinquish the property to any religious community willing to assume responsibility for the construction of a hospital. On the advice of Msgr. Joseph O'Connell of Catholic Charities in New York, Msgr. William C. Keane spoke with the Mother Provincial of the Franciscan Sisters of the Poor. Two Sisters came to Schenectady and looked over the property. The matter was taken under advisement.

In the spring of 1942, Msgr. Keane learned that Harry Furman was willing to sell 15 acres of the estate of Col. Robert Furman in the heart of Schenectady for $15,000, provided that a hospital was erected on the site. This property, known as Furman's Woods, was nearly adjacent to the Bradley Street parcel. Within one week, the Diocese of Albany advanced the money to purchase the Furman property. A "paper street" listed on maps as Beck Street separated the two properties. It was sold to the Diocese at auction, thus joining the Bradley Street and Furman parcels into a single property with frontage on McClellan Street.

In October 1942, Frank A. Dickershaid, a roofing and sheet metal worker, contacted Barney Fowler, a journalist and storyteller. Frank was troubled about the shortage of hospital beds in Schenectady. Together, they called the office of Bishop Gibbons and asked about the status of plans for a Catholic hospital. They were advised that it was still contemplated, and that a demonstration from the public was needed to set the planning in motion. After talking with various officials, Mr. Dickershaid and Mr. Fowler began to contact local priests for assistance in organizing a grass roots campaign. Msgr. Keane indicated that if 20,000 people signed petitions, it would be sufficient to move ahead.

Mr. Dickershaid drafted a petition, had it printed and began to circulate it throughout the city. At GE alone, thousands of signatures were collected. The petition highlighted the fact that Schenectady County, with a population of approximately 125,000, had only one general hospital that could not fully meet the needs of the community. It ended as follows: *"It is our understanding that the Diocese of Albany bought property in Schenectady some years ago with the intention of erecting thereon a hospital. If this is so, we respectfully urge that construction of such a hospital be started as soon as possible."* The petition also urged solid support for any associated fund-raising campaign.

The project languished during World War II, but very shortly thereafter the Bishop's office announced that the St. Clare's Hospital Campaign would begin. The notion of a new hospital mobilized the residents of Schenectady, and newspaper accounts estimated that more than 800 people joined in a kick-off rally on August 20, 1945, at the State Armory on Washington Avenue.

The fund-raising effort reached every neighborhood, large and small businesses, civic and fraternal groups, labor unions and municipal employees. Clergy of every denomination, their parishes and congregations also participated. Dr. William Gazeley, President of the County Medical Society served on the Executive Planning Committee and, along with his physician colleagues, provided advice on development of architectural drawings and plans. Community support was overwhelming.

The hospital was incorporated June 21, 1946, and a corporate board was established with Bishop Gibbons presiding. A jubilant groundbreaking ceremony took place on Oct. 26, 1946. Construction was progressing on schedule, but in April 1948, shortages of materials caused by the post-war construction boom nearly brought the project to a standstill.

The need arose for additional funds to complete construction and in April 1948, a second fund-raising campaign was launched with Henry Schaffer as chairman. By June 19, 1948, another $1.2 million had been pledged.

After nearly 2 years of construction, and at a cost of $3 million, St. Clare's was dedicated on June 13, 1948 and the cornerstone of the new, 200-bed hospital was laid by Bishop Gibbons. By September 1949, more than 4000 patients had already been admitted to the hospital, about one-half of whom received surgical care. From the beginning, the maternity service was one of the busiest in the hospital with over 700 deliveries in the first year.

The 1950s were a period of sustained growth. A new pediatrics unit opened along with a convent and chapel. A two-year school for X-ray Technologists and the region's first glaucoma detection clinic were also introduced. St. Clare's was well equipped to meet the needs of a modern hospital of the day. Facilities included x-ray machines, oxygen tents, electrocardiograph devices and an iron lung. Each hospital floor had a combination of private, semi-private rooms and wards.

During the 1960s, the hospital's school of X-ray Technology expanded and graduated nine students who completed the accelerated, two-year course. Construction began on a new building for interns, residents and medical education, located adjacent to the West Wing. It was named for Msgr. Keane, in recognition of his pivotal role in the founding of St. Clare's. Plans were also outlined for a $4-million expansion to add more medical-surgical beds, and the hospital's $500,000 emergency power system was completed.

In 1968, Jerome G. Stewart was named associate administrator—the first lay administrator in the history of St. Clare's. The following year, following the retirement of Sister Bonavita, he became Chief Executive Officer.

In 1970, there were nearly 21,000 Emergency Department visits, compared with 5800 just 10 years earlier. Similar increases in patient volume occurred throughout the hospital, creating the need for a $14-million expansion. The South-Wing expansion would add 80 private rooms on the second and third floors as well as new diagnostic and treatment centers on the lower levels. In July 1974, new patient care areas began to open, including the Critical Care Area, Emergency Department, Cardiology, X-ray and a new lobby and front entrance.

During the 1970s, the hospital introduced Total Patient Care, an innovative approach to nursing, under the leadership of Rosemary Reilly, RN, who served as Vice President of Nursing Services for 20 years. Two freestanding residencies were established: a three-year family medicine program and a one-year, general dentistry program. Many graduates of these programs have established successful practices in the area. When the newly renovated areas were dedicated in 1979, St. Clare's was more than twice its original size.

The 1980s witnessed the introduction of new technology, new campus buildings and new programs for patients of all ages. The region's first Cardiac Rehabilitation Center was launched, along with a new perspective on wellness and prevention, behavior modification and improved quality of life. This was followed by the Wellness Center, PrimeTime for Seniors, a ChildCare Center and the establishment of the St. Clare's Hospital Foundation.

The first running of the Cardiac Classic, which has become a Schenectady tradition, occurred on Thanksgiving Day in 1981, under the guidance of Dr. William Vacca, Director of Critical Care and Cardiac Rehabilitation.

Thanks to Drs. Steven Goodman and Patricia Fox, the hospital was on the cutting edge of Plastic and Reconstructive Surgery. The insulin pump, a breakthrough device for people with diabetes, made its Schenectady debut at St. Clare's under the direction of Dr. Gerardus Jameson, and the first gastroplasty—for morbid obesity—in Upstate New York, was performed by Dr. Oscar Lirio.

The decade also marked the beginning of national nursing shortages, increased marketing and advertising activity by hospitals, and growing use of computers for administrative and clinical functions.

During the 1990s, St. Clare's undertook further renovation and expansion. The Critical Care Area was upgraded, and a new lobby, registration area, ambulatory surgery center and conference center were constructed. Two new office buildings, the Health Services Building and the Cushing Center were built. The Emergency Department and the Laboratory underwent major overhauls. The Surgical Center provided a modern, comfortable environment for patients undergoing day surgery.

Several medical and surgical specialists, and service lines were added to the hospital campus. These new programs included Bariatric Surgery, comprehensive breast care, the Wound Care Center and the Sleep Disorders Center. The Capital District Dialysis Center, a pulmonary function laboratory, the Angiography Suite, and on-site child care services were also added.

The Foundation launched a capital campaign in recognition of the 50th anniversary of the founding of St. Clare's raising more than $6 million, and also introduced the Spirit of Healing Award, which was given annually to health professionals and laypersons whose work had an extraordinary impact upon the hospital and the Schenectady community.

Amidst the physical changes underway on campus, the hospital experienced a change in leadership. In 1997, Mr. Stewart retired after nearly 30 years as CEO and was succeeded by Schenectady native, Paul Chodkowski—who had actually been born at St. Clare's. Two years later, the Most Rev. Howard J. Hubbard, Bishop of the Albany Catholic Diocese, was named Chairman of the Board of Trustees, succeeding Msgr. Howard F. Manny, who retired after holding the position for 20 years.

At the same time, St. Clare's became the predominant "safety net" hospital in Schenectady, serving increasing numbers of indigent persons in the community. This trend continued into the first decade of the 21st century. A new Emergency Department opened, and visits exceeded 38,000 per year—almost double the volume of 30 years earlier. The Parish Nursing program and the School-Based Asthma Program were introduced. Plans were also developed for a new Imaging Center and an upgrade to food service facilities.

During the 2003 blackout, the largest in US history, the hospital's recently upgraded, $2.2 million backup power generating system averted a more serious crisis.

Shortly thereafter, worsening hospital finances necessitated staffing reductions. The hospital's sustainability and its future were threatened by uncompensated care for the uninsured and underinsured, and by reimbursement rates that did not adequately cover the cost of services.

In 2005, Mr. Chodkowski resigned as CEO and was succeeded by Robert Perry., who arrived two days prior to the first meeting of the Berger Commission. By then, the hospital was facing a staggering financial deficit. Despite this, St. Clare's opened the ACE Unit, providing innovative inpatient care for the elderly and upgraded its imaging facilities. Two new surgeons were recruited and the hospitalist program was expanded.

However, the hospital's grim fiscal situation weighed heavily in the final recommendations of the Berger Commission, which included closing Bellevue Woman's Hospital and joining St. Clare's and Ellis Hospitals "under a single unified governance structure."

After much discussion and negotiation, St. Clare's and Ellis announced in January 2008 that they had reached agreement on a merger. In exchange for $28.5 million from the Department of Health to fund the hospital's pension and other closing-related expenses, St. Clare's surrendered its operating license and Ellis assumed all operations at the McClellan Street campus later that year. Ultimately, the DOH agreed to allow Bellevue to remain open, also under the operating license of Ellis.

St. Clare's Hospital groundbreaking

St. Clare's Hospital, c.1950

BELLEVUE HOSPITAL

By Grace Jorgensen, MD

As the Great Depression was deepening in July of 1931, a new maternity hospital was created by and for women in the Bellevue section of Schenectady. Its founder, M. Grace Nordland Jorgensen, was a 27-year-old Registered Nurse, just five years out of Nursing school. For the next seventy years, three generations of the Jorgensen-Westney family would lead this institution.

Bellevue Woman's Hospital (now known as the Bellevue Woman's Center of Ellis Medicine) was established to meet the needs of women who had been birthing at home, at a time when women often died in childbirth. Pregnancy was viewed as an illness, and physicians did not recognize the different health care needs of women and men.

M. Grace Jorgensen's approach was novel and radical. Having given birth to her two children at home, she knew there had to be a better way. She sought to create a maternity hospital with the most up-to-date medical technology and the highest of sanitary conditions, combined with a nurturing, intimate, home-like environment. She was assisted in this endeavor by her husband, Elmer, who served as cook for staff and patients, and enforcer of medical and financial standards. "Do the right thing and do it right; only the best will do," was his credo for the center and for their children, who were happy to help, beginning at an early age.

Women across the region responded enthusiastically to the Maternity Center and, due to its success, it moved to a larger site in 1936. Its growth continued and, in 1942, it moved to its current site in the Manor, in Niskayuna, and expanded to 24 beds. With support from Elmer, daughter Grace (this writer), and son Paul, the Hospital added new health services for women, and expanded its educational programs and staff. Dr. Clarence Ackernecht and Dr. William Jameson, Sr., early supporters of the hospital, were joined by Dr. William Jameson, Jr. and Dr. Harry Wood, who served as Chief of Staff for many years. Grace Jorgensen enrolled in medical school and studied under the tutelage of noted anesthesiologist, Virginia Apgar, who developed the universal test to assess the condition of newborns. She was also a pioneer in the development of epidural anesthesia for childbirth. Dr. Apgar visited Bellevue and expressed her support for its mission. She helped Grace ensure that Bellevue would be the first hospital in the region to make this procedure available to all patients.

Upon the death of her mother in 1959, Dr. Jorgensen guided Bellevue Women's Hospital with the same commitment, dedication and sacrifice. Leading by example, she inspired the staff to help Bellevue succeed in an increasingly competitive environment. Bellevue continued to grow and became the only woman's health center in Northeastern New York to offer services in obstetrics, gynecology, infertility, neonatology and urology, with an 18-county catchment area.

In 1973, Bellevue built a $4-million addition, updating technology and becoming a forty-bed hospital. Through the persistent efforts of Rita Glavin, Esq., it became the first independent hospital in New York State to be incorporated.

In 1991, Bellevue added an eight-room ambulatory suite, a breast care center and ten private suites, enabling mothers to labor, birth and recover in a single room. That same year, Dr. Jorgensen's daughter, Dr. Clarissa Westney, joined the medical staff, representing the third generation of the founding family. Although considered small among hospitals, Bellevue achieved national recognition as "One of the 10 Best Hospitals for Women's Health Care" by Self Magazine. In a Gallup patient satisfaction survey, 99% of Bellevue's patients rated its quality of service as, "excellent" or "very good." Bellevue ranked among the top ten employers in the Capital Region for five years, and has been fully and continuously accredited by the Joint Commission on Accreditation of Health Care Organizations since its initial inspection in 1957.

In 2001, due to rising taxes, myriad mandates and regulations from more than 136 governmental agencies, and dealing with hundreds of health insurance plans, Bellevue transitioned to a not-for-profit corporation. The Hospital's operating license was transferred to Ellis in 2007, as a result of the Berger Commission.

Today, the Manor building continues to serve the health care needs of women in the Capital Region. An astounding 120,000 babies have been born at Bellevue during its seventy years, their lives a legacy of the foresight and leadership of the Jorgensen-Westney family.

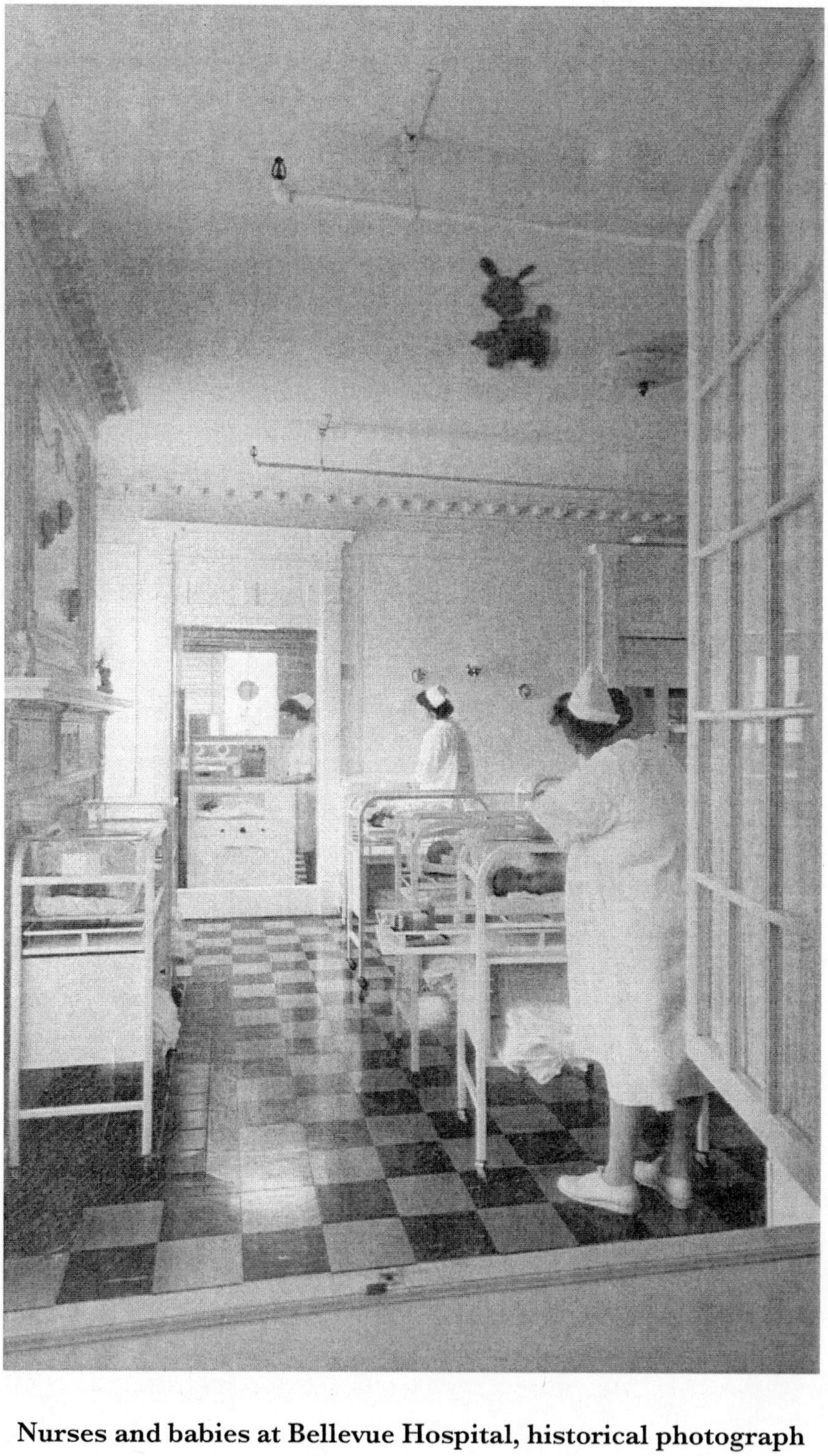

Nurses and babies at Bellevue Hospital, historical photograph

SUNNYVIEW HOSPITAL

By James M. Strosberg, MD

According to legend, Dr. Alfred Warner—an otolaryngologist—and the Schenectady Fire Chief were driving along Union Ave one day in 1925 (or thereabouts), returning from a Kiwanis meeting, when they noticed a young boy crawling along the sidewalk on his hands and knees. The child might have had one of several disorders, including polio, cerebral palsy, scoliosis, spina bifida, or tuberculosis. The sight of this unfortunate lad planted the seed of what was to become Sunnyview Hospital and Rehabilitation Center.

Under the leadership of these two Kiwanians, club members along with Schenectady firemen went door-to-door to raise funds for the construction of the "Schenectady Reconstruction Home for Crippled Children." The first patients were admitted in 1928. Later, the name was changed to "Eastern New York Rehabilitation Hospital" and, finally, to Sunnyview. Dr. William Gazely served as the first Chief-of-Staff, followed by Dr. James Holmbald. Sunnyview earned a national reputation for pediatric orthopedics such that the Mayo Clinic sent its residents to Schenectady for training. For thirty years, the hospital served only pediatric patients, many with polio and scoliosis, who sometimes stayed for years. Historical photographs show children in full body casts lying on stretchers, in front of a teacher at a blackboard in a hospital classroom.

The hospital gradually increased its number of beds and, in 1957 Dr. Robert Hoffman joined the Medical Staff as the hospital's first physiatrist. He admitted the first adult patient to Sunnyview, an admission that proved to be pivotal for the hospital's future. With the advent of the Salk and Sabin polio vaccines, and effective screening for scoliosis, the need for pediatric orthopedic rehabilitation diminished and the hospital may not have survived.

Currently, Sunnyview is licensed for 115 beds. It is one of only four freestanding rehabilitation hospitals in New York State, and serves patients from the lower Hudson Valley to the Canadian border, and from Vermont to Syracuse. Inpatient services include stroke, spinal cord injury, brain injury, amputee, orthopedic and pediatric. There is also a cardiac rehabilitation service and a pulmonary service for rehabilitation and weaning from ventilator dependence. In addition to the usual outpatient services, Sunnyview offers a nationally recognized driver re-education program, speech and hearing services, and a Wellness Center complete with a therapeutic pool.

The hospital has been a training center for students from numerous physical therapy, occupational therapy, nursing, social work, and psychology schools, as well as residents in orthopedics, physiatry, family practice, internal medicine and rheumatology.

In 2007 Sunnyview became affiliated with Northeast Health. The Sunnyview Foundation continues as a separate philanthropic entity, with its funds going only to Sunnyview Hospital.

GLENRIDGE HOSPITAL

By Richard F. Gullott, M.D. and Franklyn C. Hayford, M.D.*

Throughout the 19th century, tuberculosis was the scourge of the Western world. It affected all members of society, but was particularly unkind to the young and middle-aged. Only a third of those infected were "cured," with the rest either being condemned to death at an untimely age or suffering an attenuated life, marred by increasing infirmity due to slow progression of the disease. There were no antibiotics or effective surgical procedures that could offer hope. Famous individuals such as Chopin, Robert Louis Stevenson, Edgar Allan Poe and Tchaikovsky were among its victims.

In the latter part of the century a promising approach to treatment, that emphasized rest, became known in Switzerland. Robert Livingston Trudeau, a young New York City physician who developed active tuberculosis during his training years, retired to Saranac Lake in Upstate New York to spend his final days. Instead, he recovered and, encouraged by his own cure, which applied the Switzerland principles of isolation, congregation, rest and good nutrition, he helped launch the American sanitarium movement.

The concept grew quickly and, in 1904, Governor Theodore Roosevelt signed the public health law that supported the sanatarial movement. Quickly thereafter, every county established its own iteration of a sanatarium. There were no chest physicians or infectious disease specialists, only generalists—some of whom had been fortunate enough themselves to be cured of tuberculosis and devoted their lives to the care of others with this disease. Glenridge Sanitarium was established in Schenectady County in 1907 under the auspices of the American Red Cross, but it was incomplete—only a day camp located on Altamont Avenue at the fringe of the city limits. It consisted of an amalgamation of tents and hammocks and operated only during summertime. Prominent physicians of note who supported its establishment were Dr. Towne, Dr. Collins, Dr. Peter McPartlon, who later became the medical director, and Dr. Charles F. Clowe, whose progeny, G. Marcellus and John, each had a significant impact on medical care in Schenectady.

Throughout the State, Counties administered the tuberculosis sanitaria, and Glenridge was no exception. In 1909, a more permanent facility was established near the Aqueduct and named The Schenectady County Tuberculosis Hospital. Unfortunately, fire brought its days to an end in 1911. The second structure to be called Glenridge Sanitarium was later constructed on the site of the Lamp Farm in Glenville, and was the culmination of a two-year project beginning in 1927. Dr. McPartlon served as its first medical director until his retirement in 1933. For a period of 18 months thereafter, a staff physician, Dr. Willcox, who had distinguished himself as a productive and caring physician and administrator, was appointed superintendent by the Schenectady County Board of Legislators. Political disagreements culminated in his resignation on July 31, 1934.

James Morgan Blake, M.D. ushered in the modern era of tuberculosis treatment in Schenectady County. A victim of advanced tuberculosis, he had successfully been cured after his graduation from the University of Tennessee Medical School. He, his wife Vi, and daughter Sara-Lynn maintained a residence on the grounds during his tenure as medical director for over 44 years. During that time, Dr. Blake assembled a competent staff of specialized chest physicians, and thoracic surgeons from Albany Medical Center visited twice weekly to perform chest surgery for tuberculosis. Dr. Ehrlichman, followed by Drs. Stranahan, Alley, and Kausel, and later by Dr. Thomas Older, was responsible for the introduction of therapeutic pneumothorax, plombage, phrenic nerve crush, thoracoplasty, lobectomy, and pneumonectomy as part of the treatment armamentarium for tuberculosis at Glenridge. Dr. Blake was a renowned medical bronchoscopist, the first in the region, who later introduced the fiberoptic bronchoscope to Schenectady. In the late 1960s, Glenridge was the first institution to introduce a special care unit for post-operative and medical care of critically ill patients; Glenridge was the site of the first pulmonary angiogram in Schenectady County, as well the first clinical use of the peripheral oximeter (by Hewlett-Packard). In addition, it was an early proponent of arterial blood gas analysis with $CO2$ and Clarke electrodes, replacing the older technique of Van Slyke analysis, which was cumbersome and inefficient. This development paved the way for the modern care of ventilator patients.

Glenridge Hospital and Dr. Blake were synonymous to many, as he possessed a powerful personality. He was also politically active, held several appointments from the NYS DOH and served as President of the County and State Medical Societies.

With the introduction of streptomycin in 1944, and its active use by 1947, along with the introduction in 1952 of isoniazid, the treatment of tuberculosis changed, with pharmacologic cure becoming an attainable goal. Over the next 15 years, prolonged hospitalization for tuberculosis became a thing of the past and the need for beds at the sanitarium waned. In response, Dr. Blake was instrumental in converting Glenridge to a general chest hospital for Schenectady County, and developed the then-unoccupied nurses residence on the grounds into an active outpatient diagnostic center for medical and chest diseases. Conditions such as emphysema, chronic bronchitis, bronchiectasis, lung cancer, pulmonary fibrosis and asthma were managed aggressively, and Glenridge became a referral center that was well known throughout the state.

Upon reaching the age of 70, Dr. Blake retired in 1978 and was succeeded as medical director of by Dr. Franklin C. Hayford, previously the assistant medical director.

In the 1970s, improving technology and its availability in general hospitals, and the high costs of running a hospital, resulted in a reduction of beds at Glenridge from 122 to 60. Operations became less cost-effective and financial subsidies from the County became more difficult to secure. This resulted in political wrangling with the County Board, with encounters that were frequent and often caustic. Although Dr. Hayford instituted heroic survival measures, the County Board elected to close the hospital in December 1978. Three years later, the facilities were sold to a private corporation that converted its use to the treatment and hospitalization of individuals with addiction disorders—the present Conifer Park.

Following the closure of Glenridge, many of its physicians continued to be active in the practice of medicine or surgery.

Dr. Blake maintained a private consulting chest medicine practice in Schenectady for another 15 years. He passed away in May 2006 at the age of 98.

Dr. Hayford returned to the private practice of chest medicine for another 12 years. He later served as medical director for Mohawk Valley Medical Associates (MVMA), the physician arm of the MVP Health Plan (which was established with the support of the County Medical Society in 1982) until his retirement in 1998.

Dr. Miriam Friedenthal, director of the cardiopulmonary laboratory at Glenridge, continued in medical practice as a consultant and teaching physician in the Capital District and served as medical director of the blood gas laboratory at St. Clare's Hospital. She eventually retired to Florida.

Dr. Frank Maxon, an early staff physician at Glenridge and himself a victim of pulmonary tuberculosis, practiced chest medicine in Albany and eventually became chief of the pulmonary division at Albany Medical Center Hospital, and a mentor for many chest physicians in the region.

Dr. Joseph Denton returned to private practice after Glenridge Hospital closed but, unfortunately, became ill soon thereafter and passed away at a young age.

Dr. Ming Lee established a private practice of internal and chest medicine in Glenville, and eventually returned to Taiwan with her husband in 1998.

Dr. Lou Lasquety moved to Pensacola, Florida and practiced medicine in the armed services thereafter.

Dr. Richard Gullott continued in the practice of chest medicine in Schenectady for a number of years and later became medical director at MVMA and at St. Clare's Hospital.

Over the years, many physicians passed through the halls of Glenridge, learning skills that helped innumerable patients with tuberculosis and diseases of the chest. Many of these physicians carried their knowledge to other parts of the world. The dedication of the nursing staff, respiratory therapists, and all personnel associated with the hospital was a shining example of the highest aspirations of medicine.

* We note with sorrow the passing of Dr. Franklyn C. Hayford on October 31, 2009.

NURSING HOME BEDS

By Arnold Ritterband, MD

In 1986 and 1987, members of the Schenectady County Medical Society fought an epic battle with the New York State Department of Health, one that ended in victory for the residents of the County.

For many years, the DOH had enforced stringent certificate-of-need criteria that, among other things, restricted the supply of nursing home beds throughout the state. DOH determined the need for such beds using a theoretical bed-need formula for each county. Use of this formula resulted in a crippling shortage of nursing home beds throughout the state. On an average day in 1986, between 50 and 60 of the 413 beds at Ellis Hospital were occupied by patients waiting for placement in a nursing home. The average wait was 2 months. At the same time, a Reagan administration directive required hospitals to maintain an 80% occupancy rate for medical and surgical beds, or face severe reductions in Medicaid reimbursements along with other financial penalties.

Compounding the problem was the strange arithmetic employed by the DOH: in their counting, they disregarded beds that were occupied by patients awaiting a nursing home, and calculated the occupancy at Ellis as only 67%. It was determined that, if the hospital had closed 52 beds as demanded by the DOH, it would have operated at more than 100% capacity for 274 of 365 days in the previous year. Yet, in addition to the frequent need to place patients' beds in hallways, very sick patients were forced to wait for hours in the Emergency Department for beds in the Critical Care Unit to become available.

In November 1986, at a special meeting of the Medical-Dental Staff, the hospital administration painted a grim picture and advised shutting down the beds. But then, something unexpected occurred. Arguing that patients could not receive proper care under those conditions, the medical staff voted unanimously to urge the hospital's Board of Trustees to defy the DOH order, despite the huge financial risks.

Within 48 hours, six angry and determined physicians met to plan a strategy. The first objective, to persuade the Board to reject the administration's advice, was accomplished quickly; two Board members joined our cause. Next, the group quickly gained strength by educating itself, and by reaching out to many other physicians, as well as nurses, hospital and nursing home administrators and patients—particularly senior citizens. The group also earned the endorsement of the County Medical Society, which offered $10,000 of its funds for legal action, if necessary.

In April 1987, the group joined forces with a senior citizens' group, forming the Schenectady County Committee on Health Care Issues. Dr. John Fulco, a radiologist and former president of the County Medical Society, and Dr. Arnold Ritterband, an internist and medical activist, co-chaired the Committee. The group launched into a bitter conflict with the state Department of Health, and its commissioner, Dr. David Axelrod. Later that month, despite widespread concern about the severe shortage of nursing home beds in the Capital District, the DOH Office of Health Systems Management released a report indicating that its own calculations showed that Schenectady and Albany counties had sufficient numbers of nursing home beds. But, three months later, a New York state appellate court unexpectedly strengthened our cause. A rural, 120-bed nursing home in Upstate New York had sued the department seven years earlier for repeatedly rejecting its requests to add 80 beds. The court found for the nursing home, rejecting the Health Department's bed-need formula. Its "abstruse calculations," the court said, didn't reflect reality.

Commissioner Axelrod, however, was intransigent. In September 1987, members of our Committee met with him to seek his authorization for additional nursing home beds in the area. His response was that more beds weren't needed because many of the patients who were waiting could be cared for at home by relatives, friends and community agencies. He held to that position despite evidence from a study by his own Department that 86% of the Capital District patients waiting for nursing home placement required skilled nursing care. Moreover, many of the others would require so much care at home—if it were even available—that nursing home care would be far less costly.

Having gotten nowhere with Axelrod, the Committee turned to the N.Y. State Legislature. At our urging, a task force of Assembly Republicans held a public hearing. We recruited interested individuals and groups from all over the State to attend the hearing. Many testified that the inadequate supply of nursing home beds was causing dangerous overcrowding of emergency rooms and critical care units. Under questioning, a senior DOH official conceded that the bed-need formula, which it had been using for more than ten years, was "bizarre and arcane."

The Committee's next step was to take its message to the public—loudly, insistently and persuasively. Members of the group (including Drs. Fulco and Ritterband, Dr. Vincent Zeccola [Ellis Emergency Department], Mr. Cary Creamer, Mr. Joseph Williams, Prof. Martin Strosberg, and Assemblyman James Tedisco) appeared on radio talk shows and television news programs, spoke before county medical societies, nursing home associations and senior citizens' groups across the State. Nearly 200 news stories and editorials appeared in support of our efforts. The message was consistent: without additional nursing home beds, patients would suffer.

On Jan. 22, 1988, after a year of pressure from the committee, and a barrage of negative publicity, DOH yielded and agreed to grant a certificate of need for 160 more nursing home beds in Schenectady County. A gracious letter informing us of this decision also included thanks from the Department for our cooperation and help in the resolving the matter. This finally cleared the way for construction of the facilities needed to house the new beds.

MVP HEALTH PLAN

By Richard Lange, MD

The early 1980s witnessed the advent of Health Maintenance Organizations (HMO), a new model for health care delivery and reimbursement that was a response to the rapidly increasing health care costs of the day. Community Health Plan (CHP), which was a closed-model (or staff-model) HMO, was the first such managed care organization in the Capital Region. In such a model, physicians were employees of a "parent" corporation.

This development led the Medical Society of the County of Schenectady to explore the feasibility of forming a competing health plan that would protect and enhance the private practice of medicine and enable physicians to maintain their independence. Through this initiative, the Society was responsible for the founding of Mohawk Valley Physicians' Health Plan (now known as MVP Health Care) in 1983. After visiting several plans in the Northeast and considering several options, the Society decided to form an Independent Practice Association (IPA)-model HMO in which a physician organization would provide services to HMO subscribers through a contractual agreement with MVP. This was initially quite controversial and, in fact, considered by some to be almost communistic.

The HMO Board of Directors, comprised community leaders and physicians. (By contract, the IPA Board of Directors was an all-physician board.) Financial and administrative support was initially provided by The Lawrence Insurance Group, which agreed to provide office space and handle claims, marketing and underwriting, for which it was compensated. David Oliker was chosen as CEO after an extensive search, and MVP's success story has continued to date with Mr. Oliker still at the helm.

The plan enrolled its first members in July 1983. In due time, it was determined that it would be advantageous for the administrative functions to be handled by the HMO, and the business relationship with Mr. Lawrence and his associates concluded. MVP's initial goal was to enroll 5,000 members in the first five years, but the attraction of this model was apparently underestimated, as the plan had 50,000 members within that time frame. It expanded its operations to Utica and to Poughkeepsie and, in subsequent years, to most of New York State, with the exception of metropolitan New York City and Buffalo. Later, Vermont and New Hampshire were added. MVP now has an enrollment of 750,000 and is consistently ranked one of the best health plans in the country by sources such as US News & World Report.

In addition to growing geographically, MVP has added new product lines over the years to enhance its competitive viability. These included ASO, EPO, PPO, POS, High Deductible Plans and Government Programs. As the Plan grew, it realized that health care policy and insurance practices needed to adapt to local conditions. In 2006 a successful merger was made with Preferred Care of Rochester, with the merged entity retaining the name of MVP.

Through the years, the partnership between the IPA and the HMO has been an important component of MVP's longevity and its success in the marketplace. The size and geographic reach of the plan have far exceeded early expectations. The Medical Society is proud that MVP's headquarters remains in Schenectady, and is pleased that the plan has had a positive impact in so many other communities.

SCHENECTADY FREE CLINIC

By Arnold Ritterband, MD

The Schenectady Free Clinic opened its doors on August 7, 2003 after four years of planning. The Clinic was the brain-child of Dr. Robert Pletman, a retired urologist and member of the the County Medical Society, and of Margaret (Mardy) Moore, a civic activist. Both were members of the Board of Trustees of St. Clare's Hospital. They were deeply concerned over our national scandal: that 46 million Americans were without health insurance of any kind.

The uninsured, predominantly working poor, often get what little medical care they can from hospital emergency rooms, paying what little they can out-of-pocket; they can't afford to fill prescriptions. Care is sporadic, without adequate follow-up. Chronic illnesses such as diabetes, hypertension, coronary artery disease, asthma and depression are inadequately diagnosed and treated. One consequence is that absence of health insurance is the sixth leading cause of death in the United States.

Dr. Pletman and Ms. Moore recognized these problems, and moved to help solve them in their own community. They recruited physicians, nurses and laypersons. But, there were many obstacles to overcome. Paramount among them was the extensive regulatory burden of the NYS Department of Health. The clinic needed to operate under the aegis of a hospital, medical society or other suitable agency. Because of the expense and the enormous amount of planning needed, no such sponsoring organization could be found. Moreover, because of the proposed location in an old building, a downtown settlement house, waivers of many building and clinic regulations were needed. Multiple meetings with DOH officials suggested that, despite good intentions, some believed that their primary duty was to enforce every applicable regulation.

The other major obstacle was the provision of malpractice insurance for volunteer physicians. Some States, New York not among them, cover volunteer physicians under the State's "sovereign immunity." This regards physicians who provide care as volunteers—without reimbursement—as state employees and provides appropriate liability protection.

The sponsors of the Free Clinic devised what we believed was a solution to both problems. With help from Mr. Gerard Conway, MSSNY Senior Vice President for Governmental Affairs, a special "enabling" bill was introduced into both houses of the State Legislature. Because of opposition from some key legislators, we elected not to include a "sovereign immunity" proposal and, instead, planned to raise the money needed for malpractice insurance.

Both legislative bodies ultimately passed our bill, in different years, after long delays resulting from poor communication between Democratic and Republican leaders of the two bodies. The Assembly needed to vote again on the bill it had unanimously approved the year before. But, as the result of very late objections raised by the Chair of the Assembly Health Committee, the project suddenly seemed doomed. Rapid and difficult negotiations were then conducted with this powerful legislator.

In these negotiations, Eric Stein (our first volunteer clinic administrator); Dennis Whalen, the Deputy Health Commissioner and his principal assistants Wayne Osten and Gary LeFebre; Patricia Clancy and Molly Williams of MSSNY; Assemblyman Paul Tonko; and Paul Chodkowski, CEO of St. Clare's Hospital; played vital roles in our behalf. The Assembly passed a revised bill, requiring that we operate as an Article 28 facility, which was accepted and passed unanimously by the Senate.

Members of the Schenectady County Committee on Health Care Issues, a broad-based community group led by many Medical Society members, proved to be the final impetus for the project. One of its members, County Manager Robert McEvoy, gave the project a significant financial and psychological boost by offering $17,000 of County monies to pay for malpractice premiums. Dr. Robert Breault, a member of the Committee, and also a member of the Board of Directors of the Medical Liability Mutual Insurance Co., helped us negotiate a favorable rate for our volunteers.

The Clinic began operations at Bethesda House, but soon moved to its present location at 600 Franklin St. The Clinic cares for patients at walk-in sessions on Mondays and Thursdays, with specialty clinics on site several days a week. Services are provided by a core of some 27 volunteer physicians, 2 clinical psychologists, 23 registered nurses, 2 pharmacists and 17 other volunteers. In addition, the Clinic has had the cooperation of many of our colleagues in private practice in every specialty, who have seen, without charge, almost 2400 patients who were referred to them. The only paid staff member is our outstanding Executive Director, William Spolyar.

Thanks to our community hospitals and to Schenectady Radiology Associates, Clinic patients have received all necessary laboratory and imaging studies without charge. Moreover, the Clinic provides our patients with all prescribed medications at no cost. Some of these are donated by physicians and pharmaceutical representatives, and the majority are paid for by the Clinic, with generous assistance from Price Chopper Pharmacies.

During its first six years of operation, the Clinic had more than 21,000 patient visits, and cared for 2000-2500 (500 of whom have diabetes) of Schenectady's estimated 16,000 uninsured persons. During the fiscal year July 1, 2007 - June 30, 2008, the Clinic operated on a budget of $629,000 and delivered medical services valued at $6.4 million. Plans are afoot for Schenectady's Free Clinic to serve as a model for similar initiatives throughout the state.

ANTI-SMOKING CAMPAIGN

By Arnold Ritterband, MD

In March 1996, the Schenectady County Committee on Health Care Issues invited every physician in Schenectady to an organizational meeting for a Coalition to "wage war on smoking in our county." Its first objective was to help defeat a bill pending in the State Legislature (promoted by tobacco companies) that would have pre-empted any local government from regulating tobacco use. It was a transparent attempt to prevent cities, counties, and towns from restricting, in any way, the sale and smoking of cigarettes. The Coalition's second objective was to reduce children's access to cigarettes by removing tobacco vending machines from the County and by supporting legislation making it unlawful for merchants to sell cigarettes to minors.

The newly formed Anti-Smoking Coalition moved quickly. Defeat of the preemption bill was accomplished quickly, through the joint effort of many groups in the State, including our local Coalition. The Coalition also succeeded in achieving introduction of a resolution before the County Medical Society instructing the trustee of the Philanthropic Trust Fund to divest all tobacco company stock holdings. However, the resolution narrowly failed! Several physicians voiced the majority belief that we were improperly mixing politics with business; the Philip Morris stock held by the Fund had been highly profitable and contributed significantly to the its assets. (Within a few years, the Fund did sell its tobacco stocks.)

The Coalition, which included the Medical Society, began to focus on several tactics. These included the active promotion of "sting" operations, carried out regularly by a special unit of the Schenectady County Health Department, which were aimed at merchants selling tobacco products to children. In addition, the Coalition developed a smoking education program that was presented in the health classes of 4th-6th grades of most of the schools in Schenectady County. This program was carried out by Shelly Glock, a mother of young children and a former nursing home administrator. At the request of the Coalition, it was funded by the County Legislature beginning in 1999. Ostensibly, this program had a significant impact on the students. The program partnered with statewide and Capital District anti-smoking groups to publicize the risks of smoking. This effort was augmented by the Department of Health, which aired anti-smoking advertisements on radio and television toward.

The Coalition also encouraged all physicians to obtain smoking histories from their patients, include them as part of their recorded "vital signs," and counsel their patients to quit smoking by educating them, prescribing aids to smoking cessation, and referring them, when necessary to "quit smoking" support groups.

Much time and effort was spent to persuade the County Legislature to ban smoking in all public places, including restaurants and bars. This effort was resisted primarily by the Empire State Restaurant and Tavern Association, and it was subsequently revealed that the Association was heavily bankrolled by a group of tobacco companies. In addition, the chairman of the County Legislature was vehemently opposed, on the grounds that it would cause severe financial injury to local bars and restaurants because smokers would choose not to dine or drink out, or would do so in neighboring counties. The Coalition was in the midst of an intensive lobbying campaign when the NYS Legislature banned smoking in all public places throughout the State.

Since 1996, the local school program and anti-smoking efforts have lost traction, in part, due to a "sea change" of heightened public awareness regarding the health risks of smoking, the diminishing social acceptability of smoking and, consequently, the marked decrease in smoking rates among adults and children.

PUBLIC HEALTH SERVICES

By Martin A. Strosberg, PhD

Professor of Healthcare Management and Policy

Union Graduate College

While most New York State counties of similar size to Schenectady have long had a county health department, it was not until 1991 that Schenectady established its countywide health unit — the Schenectady County Public Health Services.

The gestation period was a long one. In 1880, the newly created New York State Board of Health recommended a countywide approach as the most effective way of handling infection and public health problems. Since the 1930s, the New York State Department of Health has been recommending and offering assistance in the creation of a county health department in all counties of the state.

Schenectady County, however, chose a different approach — a full-service City of Schenectady Health Department serving the city residents, and part-time physician Town Health Officers serving the town residents outside the city, supplemented by environmental services supplied by the New York State Department of Health District Office.

In the post-war era, many local organizations called for a consolidation of services on a countywide basis. In 1951, the Medical Society of Schenectady County voted in favor of a countywide department. In 1974, the Society reaffirmed its support in response to a feasibility study done by the Human Services Planning Council (HSPC), chaired by Elizabeth Bean. The study concluded "that the public health needs throughout the County could be more equitably, efficiently, and carefully provided under a County Health Department."

In 1988, graduate students in the Union College MBA Program in Health Systems Administration were asked by HSPC executive director, Catherine Raycroft, and Health Committee chair, Ann Smith, to update the Council's 1974 report as part of a class project. The students' analysis supported the conclusion reached 14 years earlier. At its January 1990 meeting, the Medical Society voted 23 to 21 to support the recommendation of the Union College report to form a countywide unit.

At the beginning of the decade, the time was ripe for establishment of a countywide health unit administered by Schenectady County government. The availability of increased state funding and grassroots support led by Dr. Arnold Ritterband, Dr. John Fulco, and Mr. Joe Williams, of the Schenectady County Committee on Health Care Issues, tipped the balance.

Dr. Bailius Walker of the State University at Albany was engaged by County Manager, Robert Mc Evoy, to assist in the design and development of a County Public Health Service. In 1991, the City Health Department was incorporated into a full-service county health jurisdiction.

The County hired John Cipolla as the first director. In 1992, Dr. Anne Dyson became Commissioner of Public Health, followed by Dr. Russell Fricke in 1993.

In 2009, Dr. David Pratt assumed the duties of Commissioner and his leadership was instrumental in organizing community public health efforts related to the H1N1 influenza pandemic.

TUBERCULOSIS CLINIC

By Richard F. Gullott M.D.

Tuberculosis (TB) is a serious disease. Prior to 1947, the beginning of the modern era of anti-tuberculous chemoprophylaxis, active TB was often associated with long periods of hospitalization, sometimes years. This required a sanatarial approach, which was almost exclusive to this disease. Fortunately, for each active case of tuberculosis there are 10 to 20 infected individuals who do not develop to active disease but carry the organism in their bodies in a dormant state. Some of these may become afflicted with disease later in life. It was necessary for physicians treating to address both populations, and prior to 1947, devote much of their time to the surveillance and identification of those patients who were infected, but without active disease. In 1882, Robert Koch, a German physician, identified the tuberculin skin test while searching for a vaccine for tuberculosis. Although the test never attained vaccine status, it became the gold standard with which to identify people infected with tuberculosis, but without active disease. Coupled with a chest x-ray, a diagnostic armamentarium was established that has persisted to this day.

Prior to the establishment of the Schenectady County Health Department in the early 1990s, tuberculosis identification was handled by the staff of Glenridge Sanatarium, with a number of clinics devoted to skin testing and chest x-ray procurement on the hospital site. Additionally, x-ray surveillance programs at City Hall in Schenectady were active well into the 1960s. The x-rays were transported to Glenridge, where they were interpreted with reports and recommendations sent to the local physicians. It was also common for the Glenridge staff, in conjunction with the school districts and hospitals, to provide mass tuberculin skin testing programs at these facilities each year, a task that was often monumental.

In the 1970s, after chemotherapeutic programs had become well established, and virtually eliminated the need for long hospitalizations in a specialized sanatarium, the American Thoracic Society released a report recommending that tuberculosis could be treated in general hospitals under the guidance of specially trained physicians familiar with and dedicated to the task. This nationwide paradigm shift essentially ended the sanatarial movement. Glenridge Hospital closed in 1978.

During the period of time after Glenridge was closed, and until the opening of the County Health Department, there was cooperation with various physicians and facilities, including

Ellis Hospital and Dr. Robert Tafrate, an experienced chest physician, to perform the required tasks of surveillance, identification and recommendations for care.

In 1981, the first case of AIDS was reported and, soon thereafter, it became apparent that these patients were particularly susceptible to active pulmonary tuberculosis—with dire consequences if they were not identified and treated early. Transmission of the infection to others was also a major problem. A sharp rise in active pulmonary tuberculosis, nationwide and locally, often in the milieu of multiple drug resistance, helped solidify the movement for an actively involved County Health Department in Schenectady. The County re-instituted a tuberculosis clinic. Dr. Richard F. Gullott (this author), a former staff physician at Glenridge, became chief consultant in tuberculosis for the County in 1992. The clinic was located at 650 Franklin St until its move in 2009 to quarters in the County office facility at the Annie Schaefer Center on Nott Terrace. Throughout these years, the clinic staff of nurses and administrative personnel became particularly proficient in identification, education, epidemiology, and care of patients with active and latent tuberculosis. Home care for patients, as well as directly observed medical therapy in the home and school setting is common. Close liaison with the New York State Department of Health and its Wadsworth Laboratory, and Ellis Hospital radiology and laboratory departments, has produced an efficient and effective program that has protected our County and served its citizens well. Much support from the infectious disease physicians in Schenectady, including Dr. David Rockwell and Dr. David Liebers, has resulted in quality of care that is enviable by many other counties in the State.

Technology has also aided our improved care for the tuberculosis patient. In Schenectady County, gastric lavage has given way to bronchoscopic sampling as an efficient diagnostic technique. Chest x-rays have been refined by CT scan analysis when needed. Traditional sputum smear and culture are now fortified by immunological testing of samples, enabling a reliable diagnosis long before culture reports can be verified. Most recently, the availability of quantiferon gold, an immunological blood test, holds promise for the support, or even replacement, of the traditional tuberculin skin test in the future. Additionally, and of importance, the recent development of newer medications (which may increase susceptibility to TB) for arthritis, colitis, psoriasis, and transplant patients has made the identification of early tuberculosis even more important as a public health matter.

Over the last 60 years, there have been major advances in the treatment and control of TB; nonetheless, the disease is still a major concern. Since TB affects 2 billion people worldwide, many foreign-born immigrants to the United States bring with them a new tuberculosis risk. The staff of the tuberculosis clinic, with the support of the previous Commissioner of Health, Dr. Russell A. Fricke and present Commissioner, Dr. David S. Pratt—himself a pulmonary physician, will continue to protect our community for the next decade and beyond.

GENERATIONS OF MEDICAL FAMILIES

By Lois A. Gullott

Two centuries of caring for a community is, indeed, longevity worth celebrating. Two hundred years ago, when medical societies began forming in New York State, physicians in Schenectady County were among the earliest to organize in this fashion. At that time, it is unlikely that anyone could have anticipated many of the events that would shape the history of our Medical Society, or the fact that several families would give our community three or more generations of physicians.

One such family is the Purcell family. Its medical history began with Dr. Peter Francis Purcell, who graduated from Albany Medical College in 1911. He completed his internship at Mercy Hospital, after which he opened his first office on lower Union Street and later moved to State Street. Dr. Purcell practiced General Medicine, delivered babies, made house calls, and served his country during World War I. He continued his work as a physician until his death, in 1945.

Dr. James Purcell followed in his father's footsteps, sharing his great love for medicine. In 1949, he also graduated from Albany Medical College and then completing his internship and residency at Ellis Hospital. He practiced Internal Medicine from 1955 until 1993, using his father's former office at 819 State Street. He also served his country as a physician in the United States Air Force for two years, during the Korean War.

James was among the first group of outstanding community physicians to receive the coveted St. Clare's Hospital Spirit of Healing Award. Ceil Mack, Public Relations Director for St Clare's Hospital wrote, "Dr. James Purcell will long be remembered for his outstanding and dedicated service to helping patients suffering from alcoholism and for almost three decades of work with inmates in the Schenectady County Jail."

Representing the third, and current, generation of Purcells in medicine is Dr. Peter F. Purcell. The son of James and Gertrude Purcell, the second Peter F. Purcell graduated from Cornell Medical College in 1974, and then completed his internship and residency at North Shore Hospital on Long Island. He went on to serve a fellowship in Gastroenterology at Strong Memorial Hospital in Rochester, New York, and began his Gastroenterology practice in 1979.

Dr. P. F. Purcell was also a recipient of the Spirit of Healing Award in 1997. According to Ceil Mack, "His warm friendly demeanor puts everyone at ease, his passion for medicine, family, history, scouting and an array of worthy causes makes for interesting conversation at every juncture." Peter is a Past-President of the County Medical Society and a Governor of the American College of Gastroenterology. In 2002, he was named Physician of the Year by the Crohn's and Colitis Foundation of America.

As the Medical Society enters its third century of caring, the Purcell family will soon enter its second century of service to Schenectady, and a fourth generation is on the way. Michael Wells Purcell, grandson of James Purcell and of Dr. William Wells, a retired Schenectady dermatologist, is a student at Lake Erie College of Osteopathic Medicine. Michael is scheduled to graduate in 2011, exactly 100 years after his great grandfather, Peter F. Purcell, graduated from medical school.

Another family with a distinguished record of longevity and service is the Jameson Family. Dr. William J. Jameson, Sr. was born in Schenectady in 1897, graduated from Union College and then Albany Medical College, in the class of 1921. After a rotating internship at Ellis Hospital, Dr. Jameson traveled to London to study tropical medicine. Raised with strong religious convictions and a desire to help humankind, he entered medical missionary work. Accompanied by his wife Gladys, a dietician, they traveled to the British Crown colony of Ceylon, now Sri Lanka. After completing two seven-year tours working among underprivileged people, and laboring together to bring relief to the sick and poverty-stricken of Ceylon, Mrs. Jameson kindly convinced her husband that it was time to come home to the United States to educate their children.

Upon returning in 1938, Dr. Jameson did postgraduate work at Women's Hospital in New York City and at Harvard Medical School, and entered practice in 1939. He became certified by the American Board of Obstetrics and Gynecology (Ob-Gyn) and Abdominal Surgery and was named Chief of the Department of Ob-Gyn at Ellis Hospital. He was a staff member of four area hospitals, and an assistant professor at Albany Medical College.

Dr. Jameson became very active in community organizations, serving on the Board of the Girls' Club and as Chair of the Schenectady County Medical Health Board. In 1963, Dr. Jameson was the principal donor of a cobalt unit for the treatment of cancer patients at Ellis.

Two of his sons, William Jr. and Gerardus, comprise the second generation of Jameson physicians in Schenectady. Dr. William J. (Bill) Jameson, Jr. closely followed his father's footsteps. After completing medical school, internship and residency training in New York City and Albany, he joined his father's Ob-Gyn practice. It is interesting to note that he was accompanied to Schenectady by a close friend and Brooklyn native, Dr. George Vlahides, whom he met while in school.

Bill's younger brother, Gerardus S. (Gerry) Jameson, M.D. graduated from Union College and Albany Medical College, after which he completed a fellowship in Endocrinology at the Albany Veterans' Administration Hospital. In 1963, he entered the practice of Internal Medicine and Endocrinology in Schenectady. For nearly 40 years, Dr. Jameson has provided care and guidance for thousands of patients with diabetes and other endocrine disorders. In addition, he is the assistant medical director of Glendale Nursing Home and serves as director of nursing homes for Community Hospice of Schenectady. He served with distinction as Chief of Medicine at St. Clare's Hospital for many years.

Apart from medicine, Gerry is passionate for sports. During his school days, he played soccer and lacrosse; he now enjoys tennis and is a breeder of thoroughbred horses. Speaking of his approach to patient care, Dr. Jameson said, "Somewhere along the way, you have to develop sensitivity toward your patients and their suffering, you have to be available to meet your patients needs, to provide support and to stay abreast of new technologies."

Representing the third generation of Jamesons is Dr. Gerardus L. (Lee) Jameson. Lee graduated from Albany Medical College and completed his Internal Medicine Residency and Gastroenterology Fellowship in South Carolina before returning to Schenectady. He now practices with Saratoga Schenectady Gastroenterology Associates. While considering his career choices, Lee apparently asked his father whether he would become a physician if he had to choose again. Gerry's response: "I wouldn't know what else to do."

For nearly 100 years, the Clowe family played a prominent role in health care in Schenectady, and beyond. The first records of Dr. Charles F. Clowe are traced to 1900. He served as President of the County Medical Society in 1910, became a medical missionary and moved his family to the Belgian Congo. After living and working there for several years, he and his family contracted schistosomiasis and returned home to the United States for treatment. Sadly, Dr. Clowe died prematurely of a brain tumor at age 46.

The Clowes had two sons, Harold "Doc" Clowe—who became a civil engineer, and G. Marcellus Clowe—who followed his father's career path as a physician. He practiced in Schenectady for many years, was honored by the Medical Society on the 50th Anniversary of his graduation from Medical School and lived into the 1970s.

The third Dr. Clowe, John Lee, would become the most well known. The son of Harold Clowe, John graduated from Union College and Albany Medical College and completed his internship at Ellis Hospital. He then served as a flight surgeon in the United States Air Force from 1946 to 1949. After this, he entered practice in Schenectady as a general practitioner in the 1940s. According to Larry Hart, "John has shown many talents, one being that of a soft shoe dancer who for many years directed, hosted and cajoled the Ellis Hospital School of

Nursing students to perform musical shows that lightened many hearts and raised money for nursing scholarships."

From a historical perspective, John's most significant accomplishments were in his work with organized medicine, beginning in 1974 when he served as President of the County Medical Society. He was a member of the MSSNY House of Delegates and became its Speaker. Dr. Clowe was an active member of the American Medical Association and served as Speaker of its House of Delegates. In 1991, he became President-Elect of the AMA and served as its President from 1992-1993.

Notwithstanding that three generations of physicians is a remarkable family legacy, the Kathan family surpasses that with a fourth generation. The Kathan name appears in County Medical Society records for nearly a century, and has always been associated with noteworthy accomplishments.

In his chronicle of Ellis Hospital's first hundred years, *"Hospital on the Hill,"* Schenectady historian Larry Hart writes about Dr. Dayton L. Kathan. He describes Kathan as "a typical physician in Schenectady in the 1880's—dedicated to his profession, making use of every morsel of knowledge available in that awakening era to save lives and ease suffering." After moving from Corinth to Schenectady, Dr. Kathan opened an office on Wall Street in late 1887, later moving to State Street and practiced for a half-century until his death in 1937.

Dayton had two brothers, Sherman and Wallace. Sherman was a physician in upstate New York and Wallace was a farmer in Corinth. Wallace's son, Dudley, graduated from Columbia College of Physicians and Surgeons in 1899. After practicing in Corinth for eight years, he moved to Schenectady in 1908. As was common at the time, he did not complete a formal internship and residency, but spent considerable time studying fractures in Boston, and the use of radium in Pittsburgh and New York. He made numerous trips to the Mayo Clinic applying the knowledge he gained in surgery and radiotherapy to his patients in Schenectady. Dr. Kathan spent the majority of his career as a surgeon and gynecologist. He was a soft-spoken, intelligent man who earned the confidence of his patients and the respect of his peers.

The torch was passed to Dr. Norman Kathan for the third generation. Norman was born in Corinth and moved to Schenectady as a young child. He graduated from Union College and then from Albany Medical College in 1930. Norman practiced general medicine and, later, gynecology, and served in the Army Medical Corps in the South Pacific during WWII.

He was President of the County Medical society, and of the Salvation Army, and was active with the YMCA, the Chamber of Commerce and the Schenectady Rotary. He was an active volunteer for the New York State Division of the American Cancer Society and for the Visiting Nurses Association. Dr. Kathan received an honorary degree from Union College and He was named a Patroon of the City of Schenectady in honor of his community service.

Norman and his wife, Marjorie, had three children. Their son Norman D. Kathan, Jr., (Generation Four) graduated from Albany Medical College in 1964, and, following his residency training, served in the Army for two years. He moved to New Hampshire to practice Pediatrics.

Over the past 200 years, the Schenectady community has benefited from the dedication and commitment of thousands of physicians who have served our community. On the occasion of this bicentennial, it seems especially fitting to acknowledge the work of the physicians from these four stalwart families over the past 110 years.

THE ALLIANCE

By Marie Gorman, Lois Gullott and Rose Tischler

The Auxiliary to the Medical Society of the County of Schenectady was founded in 1937. Mrs. Herman Galster and Mrs. F. Leslie Sullivan served as the first president and president-elect, respectively.

The goals of the newly-formed Auxiliary were threefold: to further the aim and purpose of the County Medical Society, to promote harmony among physicians' families, and to extend, through its members, aid to groups interested in the health and welfare of our community. These original objectives remain relevant today. In addition, the Auxiliary has supported the American Medical Association's Education and Research Foundation in its efforts to help medical schools be self-sufficient, and to avoid unnecessary government intervention in medical education.

The Auxiliary also expanded its role in community endeavors related to the public health and welfare. Significant projects included: diabetes detection education, Community Chest, Red Cross, Heart Drive, TB Seals, polio clinics, civil defense, blood bank, mental health and cancer patient transportation. Members instituted a library at the Day Hospital, offered financial aid for student nurses, and provided information about careers in health care to young people in the community. The Auxiliary worked in cooperation with the Visiting Nurses Association, assisting with sterilization of supplies and establishing a loan closet to enable those in need to obtain prescribed medical equipment.

The Auxiliary also served a social function, fostering harmonious relationships and friendships through meetings and other gatherings. Members formed bridge clubs, flower-arranging groups, bowling groups and book study clubs. Some of these activities continue today.

When the State and National organization voted to change their names, our Auxiliary also changed its name to The Alliance with the Medical Society of the County of Schenectady— often simply referred to as "The Alliance." Regardless of its name, our county organization has long been regarded as one of the strongest in the State.

Three of our past presidents went on to serve as president of the NYS Auxiliary (now, Alliance with the Medical Society of the State of New York, or AMSSNY): Mrs. Sullivan, Mrs.

Rose Tischler and Mrs. Marie Gorman. Many of our members have held other important positions, including three who served as editor of the State Alliance newsletter: Mrs. Agnes Damm, Mrs. Gorman and, most recently, Mrs. Lois Gullott. This publication, originally known as *"The Distaff,"* was renamed *"Network New York"* and then *"The Alliance Voice."*

Other active members have served on the State Board of Managers, including: Mrs. Evelyn Holmblad, Mrs. Kathy Lirio, Mrs. Janet Mae Nelson and Mrs. Stephanie Cospito. In 2010, we congratulate Stephanie Cospito on being installed as AMSSNY Co-President Elect, and also Amy DiCaprio as Recording Secretary, Cheryl Stier as Co-Chair of Health Promotions, and Helena Mirza and Amy DiCaprio as members of the Nominating Committee. We are proud that these members have taken leadership roles at the State level.

Over the years, our Alliance has become politically active, lobbying in Albany against all medical-related bills that the State Medical Society deemed undesirable, and advocating for those the Society endorsed. Alliance members attended legislative sessions and sent personal messages to State and Federal officials. These same members became proponents for community education by presenting relevant information to their fellow Schenectadians.

Our programs and projects are responsive to the important issues of the day. When the nursing shortage was identified, a few years ago, the Alliance established nursing scholarships—based on need and academic merit—for second year students at the Ellis Hospital School of Nursing. Our Alliance Memorial Loan Fund, established more than 40 years ago, provides interest-free loans to students entering health-related fields of study. These two projects and our yearly donations to selected not-for-profit organizations are supported by our philanthropic fund-raising efforts.

Today, our Community Health Education Committee remains the strongest part of our Alliance. This Committee promotes health education and awareness to students in our area schools. One of our newer projects is S.A.V.E. Day (Stop America's Violence Everywhere). This program was initiated by the AMA Alliance, which has designated the second Wednesday in October as S.A.V.E. Day. To help encourage non-violent behavior and non-violent conflict resolution, members have enlisted area schools to distribute books and instruct youngsters using materials developed by the AMA Alliance, such as *"Hands Are Not for Hitting"* and *"Dealing with Bullying."* These programs have been very well received.

One of our most recent, and most successful, programs has been the distribution of *"Think, Don't Drink"* cards. Initiated in Schenectady County by our Alliance, and now used statewide, this program is intended to make teenagers aware of the dangers of drinking and driving especially, during prom season. The Alliance, in partnership with Price Chopper Supermarkets' Floral Departments across New York, distribute these cards in prom flower containers to remind teens to think first of safety for themselves and their friends. Beginning five years ago with 500 cards in Schenectady County, we now deliver 11,000 throughout New York State through Price Chopper stores.

Throughout the years, our Alliance has always been ready and willing to assist our County Medical Society in its service to Schenectady. We are proud of our history and of our innovative programs and projects. We continue to address the health challenges of today and try to anticipate those of of the future. We are a unique group of Physician Spouses, whose mission is to help improve the health and welfare of the community. Moving forward, we will remain resolute in our commitment to this mission.

CARDIOLOGY

By John Nolan, MD

Forty years ago, Cardiology in Schenectady involved little more than the use of a stethoscope and an electrocardiogram by internists and family physicians. However, a transformation occurred during the 1970s, thanks to the efforts of several physicians who have come to be remembered as the pioneers of Cardiology in Schenectady. They include: Drs. Maurice Donovan, Morris Shapiro, Francis Giknis, Kanakaiahnavara (Ken) Shankar and Gerald Matura. They brought a new level of expertise to the treatment of cardiovascular diseases and were instrumental in the development of Coronary Care units at Ellis and St. Clare's Hospitals. These units resulted in a dramatic decrease in deaths due to one of the most serious public health problems—acute myocardial infarction (MI, or heart attack).

The early 1980's brought another new era—a wave of university-trained, board-certified cardiologists with expertise in cardiac ultrasound and invasive cardiology, including coronary angiography. These physicians included Drs. Jack Siegel, Paul Dworkin, William Vacca, John Nolan (this author), and Barry Lindenberg. Thanks, in part, to the expertise of these physicians, Ellis developed a freestanding Critical Care fellowship program, and St. Clare's expanded its Critical Care Area. By 1990, several Cardiology practices merged to form one large group, known as Cardiology Associates of Schenectady. The nine founding members included Drs. Nolan, Lindenberg, Dworkin, Robert Parkes, Arthur Vakiener, Douglas Long, Denis Manor, David Armenia, and the late Edward Wright.

This group, and its capacity for coronary intervention, provided the impetus for development of an open-heart surgery program at Ellis. This center of excellence continues today. Dr. Thomas Older, the chief of Cardiothoracic Surgery at Albany Medical Center, was recruited to be the first Chief of Cardiac Surgery at Ellis, and was joined by Dr. Harry DePan, who later succeeded him as Chief. The program grew quickly, performing about seven hundred open-heart surgeries per year. All types of cardiac surgery, including coronary bypass, valve and aortic root replacement, and valve repair were performed with great expertise and excellent clinical outcomes. At the same time, Dr. Wright, began a percutaneous coronary intervention and angioplasty program, which would grow under the leadership of Dr. Parkes to serve almost 600 patients per year.

Soon thereafter, Dr. George Vassolas was recruited from the Lahey Clinic to serve as head of the new electrophysiology (EP) program at Ellis, where he was later joined by Dr. Robert Joy. With many technological advancements, the EP program has expanded its scope from pacemakers, to include ablations, treatment of arrhythmias, and prevention of sudden death through implantation of automatic cardiac defibrillators. Most recently, the EP program has implemented device therapy for patients with severe congestive heart failure.

In 1993, Dr. Nolan was appointed Chief of Cardiology and continues in that capacity today. Wishing to foster a team approach to cardiac care, he formed the Department of Cardiovascular Sciences in 1996, which united the various subspecialties of cardiology and cardiac surgery. This enabled department members to collaborate in developing and improving cardiovascular services for the benefit of the community. The department now comprises 22 cardiologists, three cardiac surgeons and 8 physician assistants and serves Fulton, Montgomery and Southern Saratoga Counties, in addition to Schenectady.

With the recent development of the STEMI Program, targeted toward patients with certain types of heart attacks, there has been a further decline in deaths due to acute myocardial infarctions. This program has been championed by Dr. Joy and Dr. Steven Weitz, with the assistance of the staff in the Cardiac Catheterization Laboratory. In addition, under the direction of Drs. Parkes, Weitz, Mark Jordan and Peter Cospito, improved techniques in percutaneous coronary revascularization have greatly reduced the need for coronary bypass. Now, many patients can avoid the pain and long recuperation associated with open-heart surgery.

At the end of the first decade of the 21st century, we can look back with satisfaction at these accomplishments. The future looks much brighter than we could have imagined forty years ago, when the death rate from acute MI was 30%, compared with 5% or less at Ellis Hospital today. We look forward to further reduction in the burden of heart disease as our preventive measures become more effective: raising awareness of the importance of eating well, avoiding tobacco use, exercising regularly, and controlling cardiovascular risk factors such as high blood pressure and diabetes.

ORTHOPAEDICS

By James E. Holmblad, MD

For nearly 90 years, the Schenectady medical community, and the community-at-large, have been served by orthopaedic surgeons renowned for their clinical and surgical skills. A brief chronicle of Schenectady's orthopaedists follows.

When Schenectady's rehabilitation hospital (now known as Sunnyview) was founded in 1928 by Dr. A. Warner and community supporters, it became apparent that orthopaedic surgery would be integral to patient care. Dr. William Gazeley had taken an interest in the initiative in 1925 and decided to join Dr. Warner in caring for children in the hospital. Gazeley performed orthopaedic surgery and became the hospital's first chief of staff.

In 1939, Dr. Donald MacElroy joined the practice of Dr. Edward Cravener, who was performing some orthopaedic surgery. The same year, Dr. Louis Cohen came to Schenectady and opened his practice of orthopaedic and trauma surgery. Dr. W.A. Dunham joined Dr. Gazeley's practice and, during World War II, gained much experience in the treatment of fractures.

After the war, Dr. George Reich began to practice orthopaedic surgery, with a focus on patients with cerebral palsy. The Ellis Hospital Orthopedic Surgery Residency also began at around this time. It comprised four residents from the early 1950s into the 1960 and continues with three residents today. Dr. James Holmblad (this author) was a resident from 1951-52 in Children's Orthopaediccs, after which he joined Drs. Gazeley and Dunham in their practice.

Several specialists visited throughout the year to see patients with specific problems: Dr. John Cobb for scoliosis, Dr. J. William Littler for hand surgery, and Dr. Joseph Godfrey for children. At around this time, Dr. Mario Bonaquist settled in Schenectady after his residency training and was joined later by Dr. Anthony Guidarelli. Following Dr. Bonaquist's retirement, Dr. Guidarelli remained in solo practice.

Dr. James Nelson joined Drs. Gazeley, Dunham, and Holmblad after his residency at Mayo Clinic, during which he spent six months at Sunnyview Hospital. However, Drs. Dunham and Holmblad later left Drs. Gazeley and Nelson to form their own practice in 1968. In the ensuing years, they were joined by Dr. John Spring, Dr. John Richards, and Dr. Gary Williams. This practice became known as Schenectady Orthopaedic Associates, and Dr. Richard D'Ascoli joined the group shortly thereafter.

Meanwhile, Dr. Carl Paulsen became associated with Drs. Gazeley and Nelson, and they were joined by Dr. Patrick Albano. This group was known as Rosa Road Orthopaedics, and they were joined by Dr. Robert Leupold, Dr. Robert Cooley, Dr. James Smith and Dr. Rory Wood.

Dr. Spring performed the first total hip replacement in Schenectady in 1972 after taking instruction from Dr. William Harris in Boston. Dr. Paulsen began performing the procedure later that year.

Dr. Shashi Patel was in solo practice for many years but later joined Schenectady Orthpaedic Associates.

Responding to pressures in the financial and regulatory environment, Rosa Road Orthopaedic Associates and Schenectady Orthopaedic Associates merged in 1996 to form Schenectady Regional Orthopaedic Associates (SROA). They renovated a large building on Liberty Street, and the practice remains situated at that location. The original members of SROA included Drs. Albano, Cooley, D'Ascoli, Holmblad, Leupold, Paulsen, Patel, Richards, Smith, Spring, Williams, and Wood.

Over the last several years, Drs. Eric Aronowitz, James Boler, David Bowman, and Matthew DiCaprio have joined the group. Each physician has one or more areas of interest or advanced training, enabling SROA to offer the Schenectady community a full range of orthopaedic consultation and surgery.

RADIOLOGY AND MEDICAL IMAGING

By John D. Fulco, M.D., FACR, FSIR, FAHA

Over the past sixty years, technological developments in Radiology and Medical Imaging have reshaped the diagnosis and treatment of many illnesses. These advances transformed Radiology from an experimental curiosity in the early 20th century to a complex and sophisticated, computer-based science.

It is believed that the first radiographs in Schenectady were demonstrated in 1898 by Dr. Charles F. Clowe, showing fractures of the forearm. Since that time, radiology has evolved to include organ-based imaging and a full spectrum of therapeutic applications. The modern era of Radiology in Schenectady began after World War II, when many general practitioners returned from military service and entered specialty training. Its story is one of individuals, of groups and of facilities.

At that time, several radiologists worked on their own, in solo or small private practices. Dr. Moses Sommer, a prominent radiologist at that time, graduated from the University of Lyons, in France. He maintained a private practice for his entire career, in addition to providing some services to the hospitals.

Dr. Elmer St. John, a graduate of AMC, had a private practice in Downtown Schenectady. He had an interest in radiography of domestic animals. Before the specialty of Diagnostic Veterinary Radiology was established, he worked at animal hospitals in the Capital District, performing gallbladder series and barium studies, and interpreting plain radiographs on dogs and cats, and—less commonly—on cows and horses.

Beginning with the post-war era, imaging services at Bellevue Hospital were provided primarily by part-time radiologists until the early 1980s. Dr. Edward DeFeo practiced at Bellevue and Ellis (and later, St. Clare's). He graduated from Union College in 1941 and the University of St. Louis School of Medicine in 1944. Dr. DeFeo completed residency programs in Brooklyn and Chicago, and at the National Institutes of Health.

After the arrival of Dr. Thomas Frede from the Albany VA Hospital in about 1983, the ultrasound equipment was upgraded and expanded imaging services for Obstetrics and Gynecology were established. Dr. Frede was joined by Dr. Brad Ruthberg in 1986, and by Dr. Judith Ruthberg in 1987. Mammography services expanded, and a mobile mammography unit became a symbol of Bellevue's outreach. The staff would later expand to include Dr. Tariq Gill and his colleagues from Millenium Medical Imaging, as well as Dr. Mussarat Chaudhry, who provided professional services on a per diem basis. In the aftermath of the Berger Commission, members of Schenectady Radiologists, PC (SRPC) also began working at Bellevue.

At Sunnyview, multiple part-time radiologists provided services from the 1940s through the 1960s. Dr. Edward Defeo was on staff until the early 1970s, and Dr. Kencil Mitton joined in April of 1971. Mitton was a graduate of the University of Western Ontario. He completed his radiology residency at Victoria Hospital and Memorial Children's Hospital in London, Ontario and was associated with the Cornell University Radiology department after leaving Canada. After coming to the Capital District, he joined the Radiology department at Albany Medical Center (AMC). He also had a private practice on State Street, in downtown Schenectady, and provided services to the clinic at General Electric. He was joined in 1971 by Dr. Anthony Tabacco, a graduate of AMC who also practiced in Albany.

In 1976, Dr. Edward McCabe became the primary radiologist at Sunnyview. He provided services in general radiology, with a strong commitment to the imaging of bones and joints. In addition, the department provided barium studies, venography, intravenous pyelography and arthrography. More modern services, such as videofluoroscopy, bone densitometry and duplex ultrasound were added later, under the guidance of radiologists from SRPC. Dr. John Fulco (this author) served as the first Chief of Radiology, until 1992. He was succeeded by Dr. Leonides Fernando, and—in 2008—by Dr. Marvin Schwartz.

As one would expect, most of the radiology services in Schenectady have been provided at St. Clare's and Ellis hospitals. Dr. Sommer continued to work on a part-time basis at St. Clare's until a more coverage was needed and the hospital hired Dr. Harold Curran, who had been an x-ray technologist during World War II. After the war, he enrolled in New York Medical College, graduated in 1952 and came to Schenectady after completing his Radiology residency. He served as Chief of Radiology from 1960-1985, during which time he recruited Drs. John Gorman and Donald Morton. Dr. Gorman completed his residency in Syracuse in 1962, followed by a fellowship at AMC, where he served as an attending radiologist before coming to St. Clare's. Dr. Morton was born in Maine and schooled at the University of Vermont. His Radiology residency was at AMC, and he served briefly there as an attending radiologist before joining his colleagues in Schenectady and forming Old Dorp Radiology, PC.

St. Clare's installed its first CT scanner in 1980, which was only capable of head scans until it was upgraded to a body scanner in the mid 1980s. The hospital's first MRI arrived in 1998. In 2000, St. Clare's added a multi-disciplinary Vascular and Interventional Radiology suite. However, this service was a victim of budget cuts and it closed in 2007. Currently, the Ellis

Health Center (located at the former St. Clare's site) operates a 16-slice GE CT scanner and a mid-range MRI. Mammography for the entire Ellis Medicine health system is performed at the Bellevue and McClellan Street locations.

At Ellis, Dr. DeFeo served as Chief of Radiology from 1960-1973. He was the founder and first president of the Northeastern New York (NENY) Radiology Society and of Schenectady Radiologists, PC. Dr. Defeo was a musician, an avid sailor and a competitive tennis player. He was joined in the mid-1960s by Dr. Charles Stamm, following completion of his Residency in Ann Arbor, Michigan. He also served as president of the NENY Radiology Society and as its treasurer. In the 1970s, the Radiology Department moved to new and expanded quarters and added Drs. Herbert Reilly, John Snell, Leonard Meiselman and Joseph Asaro. The new department featured upgraded ultrasound facilities, polytomography, head CT and a new angiography suite.

Drs. Stamm and Reilly practiced General Radiology, and were active in the community, and both were involved in the Schenectady Symphony Orchestra. Dr. Stamm became Chairman of the department in the 1970's, followed by Dr. Reilly. Dr. Asaro took a circuitous route to Schenectady, graduating from Medical School in Palermo, Italy, completing his residency on Long Island (NY), and working in the military in Washington State and at West Virginia Medical Center before joining the department at Ellis. His areas of interest were mammography and breast ultrasound.

Dr. Meiselman, the first angiographer at Ellis, was a graduate of SUNY Downstate Medical Center in Brooklyn. He completed his residency in Chicago and practiced in New Jersey before coming to Schenectady. Angiography was practiced in Schenectady by three specialties, including Neurosurgery, Vascular Surgery and Radiology, each of which approached the procedure somewhat differently. Drs. Thomas Mason and Gerald Haines (Neurosurgeons) performed cannulation of the carotid arteries. Drs. Robert Blumenberg and Michael Gelfand (Vascular Surgeons) performed translumbar aortograms with a rigid needle inserted into the abdominal aorta.

In 1979, Dr. Fulco was the first at Ellis to perform catheter-based angiography of the abdominal aorta and its branches, the brachiocephalic arteries and the cerebral circulation. This technology was followed by balloon angioplasty of the renal and peripheral arteries, as well as stenting, thrombolysis, and embolotherapies—all of which helped reduce the need for more invasive surgical treatment of a number of serious conditions. Similarly, the percutaneous placement of venous filters through the inferior vena cava replaced surgical cut-downs. Later, image-guided biopsies and drainage procedures, including paracentesis and thoracentesis became available.

Dr. Fulco was followed by a number of other fellowship-trained radiologists, including Drs. Gary Wood, Leonides Fernando, Michael Burke, Eric Wagle, Marvin Schwartz, Sasi Cheruvu and Angel Fermin. The two Radiology groups eventually merged, enabling SRPC to provide services at Ellis, St. Clare's and Sunnyview. The newly expanded group also included Drs. Juho Song, Jay Malde, Areta Pidwerbetsky and Joseph Pazienza. SRPC opened a freestanding imaging facility, Balltown Imaging Center, in June 1990, and a second facility, Guilderland Imaging Center, followed about 15 years later. Each of these centers offers a full range of imaging studies, including radiography, CT, MRI, mammography and ultrasound.

During the 1980s, Ellis acquired a diagnostic ultrasound unit for ophthalmology and a real-time ultrasound scanner for assessing cerebral blood flow. Digital subtraction angiography also became available, enabling precise images of large blood vessels throughout the body, using only an intravenous contrast injection. In the late 1980s a General Electric, 1.8-Tesla, high-field MRI was installed. Drs. Wood and Fernando worked in collaboration with GE engineers and technologists to improve the capabilities of MRI.

Drs. Wood and Fernando, neuroradiologists, performed myelography and discograms, as well as epidural and facet injections for pain management. They also established a weekly, multi-disciplinary Neuroscience conference involving the departments of Pathology, Neurology, Neurosurgery and Radiology. Dr. Wood was elected Chairman of the Ellis Radiology Department in 1991 and served in that capacity until 2006. The use of angiography, as well as therapeutic and interventional procedures, grew during this time, and the CT was upgraded to a 64-slice scanner. A second, 8-slice scanner was added for biopsies and CT-guided interventional procedures.

Dr. Fulco trained at Tufts-New England Medical Center in Boston and at the Long Island Jewish–Hillside Medical center and the Queens Medical Center in New York City.

Dr. Burke completed an Internal Medicine residency in the early 1980s, prior to his residency in Diagnostic Radiology, and he served as an attending radiologist at Albany Medical Center from 1989-92, before coming to Schenectady. Dr. Burke was elected Chairman of the Ellis Radiology Department in 2006, and was re-elected in 2008. He has been instrumental in expanding and upgrading the PACS system, which uses electronic technology to store and share medical imaging studies. In addition, CT colonography was introduced and Nuclear Medicine services were expanded (see below) during his tenure.

Dr. Fernando completed his residency in Diagnostic Radiology at St. Peter's Hospital in Alblany, followed by a fellowship in Neuroradiology at Albany Medical Center. He and Dr. Wood staff a pain management program at the Spine Center in Latham, in addition to their imaging activities.

Dr. Malde completed post-graduate training in Radiology at Bridgeport (CT) Hospital and at the University of Pittsburgh Medical Center. Dr. Cheruvu graduated from the SUNY Buffalo School of Medicine and Biomedical Science prior to his residency in Diagnostic Radiology.

Dr. Pazienza graduated from Albany Medical College and also completed his residency in Diagnostic Radiology in Albany. He became medical director of the Balltown Imaging Center in the early 1990's and coordinates interpretation of imaging studies for the New York Oncology and Hematology office in Rexford.

Dr. Pidwerbetsky has focused her efforts on breast imaging, including mammography, ultrasound and MRI. She was the recipient of the 2009 Jane Golub award for excellence in women's health, and served as Chair of the Department of Medical Imaging at St. Clare's until the merger with Ellis. Drs. Wagle and Schwartz are the principal diagnostic radiologists at the Guilderland Imaging Center. Dr. Wagle is also an alumnus of Albany Medical College and its Diagnostic Radiology residency. He completed a fellowship in MRI at the University of Maryland. Dr. Schwartz is a graduate of New York Medical College, and completed his residency in Diagnostic Radiology at Morristown (NJ) Memorial Hospital followed by a fellowship in Albany.

Dr. Song was on staff at Auburn (NY) Memorial Hospital prior to serving a Fellowship in Vascular and Interventional Radiology at AMC. Dr. Fermin completed his residency in Diagnostic Radiology as well as fellowships in MRI, Ultrasound and CT at Albany Medical Center. He served as Chief of Radiology at the Albany Veterans' Administration Hospital before coming to Schenectady.

Many of the radiologists were active in hospital leadership, community affairs and organized medicine. Notably, Dr. Meiselman was a founding member of the Mohawk Valley Physicians Health Plan, and later served as Chairman of the board. Drs. Fulco and Wood served as Chief of Staff at Ellis, and on the hospital's Board of Trustees. Dr. Fernando was also a Trustee and served the Hospital Foundation during several major fund-raising efforts including renovations of the Emergency Department and construction of the Bruggeman Center for ambulatory services.

Dr. Wood currently serves on the Board of Censors of the County Medical Society and is the president and managing partner of SRPC. He and Dr. Fernando are authors of numerous publications in the Neuroradiology literature, including case reports and research studies. In addition, they have contributed to advancement of diagnostic and therapeutic neuroradiology at Ellis, including the diagnosis of stroke, cerebral thrombolytic therapy and the percutaneous management of neurogenic pain. Drs. Burke and Wood established a teleradiology service at all 3 hospital campuses to cover night readings from the hospital system and the emergency departments.

Dr. Fulco is a past-president of the Medical Society and of the Fourth District Branch of MSSNY. He has been an active leader in the Society of Interventional Radiology and served as Chair of the AMA's Section Council on Radiology. Dr. Fulco and Dr. Arnold Ritterband are the co-founders of the Schenectady County Committee on Health Care Issues and is a member of the Board of Directors of Mohawk Valley Medical Associates.

*   *   *

Apart from Radiology, Schenectady has a long history of imaging services using modalities in Nuclear Medicine, beginning with Dr. Hans Rozendaal. A native of the Netherlands, he served in the US military and worked for several years at the Mayo Clinic. After World War II, he became manager of the Division of Life Sciences Studies at the Knolls Atomic Power Laboratory in Niskayuna. He began his private practice of Nuclear Medicine in 1965 and was joined that same year by Dr. Richard H. Lange. After Dr. Rozendaal's retirement, Dr. Lange shared call and coverage with Dr. John Shields, who practiced Nuclear Medicine at St. Clare's until his retirement in 1991. Following Dr. Lange's retirement a year later, Nuclear Medicine services were provided by SRPC. Diagnostic equipment underwent a major upgrade in 2003 and expanded with the transfer of a gamma camera from St. Clare's in 2008.

Dr. Lange was very active in organized medicine and community affairs, including the American Cancer Society and the Schenectady Red Cross. He was a charter member of the Ellis Hospital Foundation and a founding member of the Mohawk Valley Physicians Health Plan, later serving as its medical director.

*   *   *

Future plans for imaging services in Schenectady include acquisition of a PET scanner and the anticipated need for expansion of facilities to accommodate increasing demand for angiography and interventional studies. New developments in molecular imaging, radioisotopes, more powerful MRI units, radiofrequency and cryoablation and the nanoknife hold much promise for improving the precision and sophistication of imaging studies in the years to come.

POEM

By Christine Parkhurst Moore, MD

Gerald Parkhurst MD, Past President of the Medical Society and Past Chief of Pathology, worked at Ellis Hospital for 21 years. During his tenure, he maintained an independent pathology residency and also a school of medical technology. He received his medical degree from the University of Vermont and trained at the Mallory Institute of Pathology. He was a Board Member of Ellis Hospital and Past President of the Medical-Dental Staff. Gerry was a man of absolute integrity respected by all who knew him. Dr. Parkhurst died in 1983. He gave freely of his talents and fellowship to his colleagues and friends.

His daughter, Dr. Christine Parkhurst Moore, wrote this poem in his memory.

CHARON

Sometimes Dad wasn't ready to come home yet
So I wandered around his office, tapping the glass
To watch the guppies move through the weed
And reading posters about Harvey and Alzheimer,
Cox, Archibald Smith

Then down the silent familiar hall
That smelled like pickles and insecticide
To see the other fishtanks:
The fetus contemplating its umbilicus,
The tapeworm folded over and over
Like an enormous egg noodle,
The cafe coronary trachea
With its bite of steak still lodged

And past the always closed door
To the room of last answers
This adult male, a brain bleed
That elderly woman
So many milligrams of what sedative
That young girl
Exsanguination
Secondary to shame
Secrets discovered

And kept on file in the quiet library down the hall
The library of bound volumes, final report cards
External genitalia (normal)
Internal organs (weight, appearance)
Blood levels (too high, too low)

And here they sit in dusty green leather
Old and old and young
Finished, no more to report, ever
Back in my father's office
I look through the microscope
At the beginning of the journey
That ends in the library
Fields of beautiful blue and magenta cells
There, see, look at eleven o'clock,
Toward the center, the one that's wrong
The new growth that's beginning to blossom

The same growth that bloomed in my father
After years of breathing formaldehyde
Years of breathing the secrets
Of cells, of sorrow, of cosmic entropy
He died, and had his body burned
No autopsy, no library
To ashes, to dust, to nothing
Released

BIOGRAPHIES

This section is devoted to brief biographical sketches of several physicians who have contributed in remarkable ways to health care in Schenectady during the past fifty years.

Lawrence A. Cioffi, MD

By Cristine Cioffi, Esq.*

Known to his friends as "Chic," Dr. Cioffi overcame disproportionate social odds to become a respected physician in Schenectady, ultimately serving as Chair of the Department of Obstetrics and Gynecology at Ellis Hospital. Born to immigrant parents, he was the first person in his family to graduate from high school, in Troy, New York. He attended St. Lawrence University where, initially, he lived in the unheated attic of a freshman dormitory while the maintenance staff looked the other way.

After graduating from college early, he attended Officer Training School and served in the Navy aboard the USS Hancock. Following World War II, he entered Albany Medical College. He served his internship and residency at St. Clare's Hospital and at Ellis, respectively. With his new wife, Helen Morse Cioffi, serving as receptionist, nurse, bookkeeper and housekeeping staff at his first office on Sacandaga Road in Scotia, he built a thriving practice and a storybook marriage.

As a staff physician at Ellis and St. Clare's, he participated in the teaching and mentoring of several generations of physicians—an opportunity he relished. He also lectured at the Ellis Hospital School of Nursing. Dr. Cioffi, while small in stature, had enormous compassion and extended much generosity toward his patients. Many nights, he would stay on long past his designated time on call in the labor and delivery suite, to see a patient through the birth of her child.

Helen and Chic, together, forged a partnership that also resulted in three children and eight grandchildren. Dr. Cioffi's patients, his marriage and his family meant the world to him. He died several days short of his 87th birthday, after a long illness.

* Cristine Cioffi is the daughter of Helen and Lawrence Cioffi and currently Chairs the Ellis Hospital Board of Trustees.

*　　*　　*

Henry E. Damm, MD

By Louis S. Snitkoff, MD, FACP*

Dr. Henry Damm began his practice in 1953 as a General Practitioner, or GP. At that time, the GP was the "family doctor," called upon to treat illness, deliver babies, suture lacerations and offer counsel to patients during times of physical, psychosocial and spiritual stress.

Dr. Damm was a veteran of World War II, serving in the North Atlantic. He then attended Union College in Schenectady and graduated in 1948, after which he graduated from Albany Medical College in 1952. He married Agnes Mullin and they became the parents of four daughters—Deborah, Elizabeth, Nancy and Donna—and a son, Henry Jr.

During his 45 years as a Schenectady physician, Dr. Damm had a particular affinity for St. Clare's Hospital because of its smaller and more intimate feel, its loyal staff, and its mission of healing under the aegis of the Catholic Church. After 30 years in private practice, he devoted his full time and effort to the Hospital. He was a longstanding member of the St. Clare's Board of Trustees, Director of its Family Practice Residency Program, Director of Medical Education and Vice President for Medical Affairs. Dr. Damm was a recipient of the St. Clare's Spirit of Healing Award and the St. Clare's Hospital Founders Medal. He also served for many years on the Medical Staff Executive Committee at Sunnyview Hospital.

Sometimes perceived as a bit gruff and having a no-nonsense demeanor, Henry was really a "people person," and patients viewed him as a member of the family. He made regular home visits in addition to his hospital rounds and office hours. He was a terrific listener, and learned much about carpentry, plumbing, boats and many other subjects from talking with his patients. He came to know them and their families and, in turn, each of his daughters worked in the office through high school.

In addition to his family and his career, Henry had a passion for food—especially Mediterranean food. His patients knew this, and when they were financially strapped, they would always remember him with tomatoes, sweet corn, hot Italian peppers, zucchini, homemade sauces and Baklava.

Dr. Damm retired from St. Clare's Hospital in 1997 and passed away on September 25, 2001 following a lengthy illness.

*The author is grateful to Deborah Damm O'Brien and Elizabeth Cole, daughters of Henry and Agnes Damm, who contributed information to this biography.

*　　*　　*

Thomas Oram, MD

Tom Oram was one of the most colorful figures in recent memory to have been a member of the Medical Society of the County of Schenectady. His father was a medical officer in the British Army and Tom lived all over the world. He was the only physician to serve as Chief Resident in Medicine as well as Chief Resident in Pathology at Ellis Hosptial. Dr. Oram directed a 50-bed hospital in Vietnam during the war. He taught Parasitology at Albany Medical College and served as President of the Medical Society. During each of the 22 years in which the Ellis Medical-Dental Staff held its Annual Scientific Day, he contributed a most interesting talk that was didactic as well as entertaining.

The following is excerpted and adapted from remarks written and delivered by Dr. N. Balasubramaniam, also a Past-President of the Medical Society, on the occasion of Dr. Oram's retirement. (James M. Strosberg, MD)

I have personally known Dr. Oram for about 33 years, first as a teacher, then as Chairman of the Pathology Department and finally as a colleague. He was a pathologist, Director of the laboratory and the residency program in pathology and, finally, a Medical Examiner.

I believe that Heaven and Hell are not 'out there.' They are in the hearts of men and women. Heaven is in the hearts of men like Dr. Thomas Oram. I know of no greater cause than the ability to relieve human pain and suffering.

Pathology is not merely making a diagnosis or, in the case of the Medical Examiner, doing autopsies and signing death certificates. Dr. Oram has taught all his life. Every time I spoke with him, I always learned something new, either about medicine, religion, philosophy, history, politics and, of course, about food and the British Empire.

Helping families cope with tragic situations is an art by itself. I almost feel that there may be a gene for it, and Dr. Oram had it. In the Medical Examiner's world, death is almost always sudden, and I have seen first hand his rare ability to console individuals and, in some cases, to diffuse potentially explosive situations, fraught with complex medicolegal issues.

When I called him by phone, he never once told me "I will call you back." He was always available, and that made my life as a pathologist infinitely better. Over a span of 30 years, I have never seen him angry.

Greatness in life, in my opinion, comes not from winning the Nobel Prize, or by becoming a president. Greatness comes from helping others, from always being content and from having a cheerful, smiling face; by these criteria, Dr. Oram was a great man.

Sir Winston Churchill said, "Accepting responsibility for others is true greatness." Dr. Oram made this philosophy a constant refrain in all of his actions. For the past 30 or more years Dr. Oram has gone out of his way to meet with families, law enforcement agencies and legal professionals to maintain a cordial and, most importantly, respectful relationship with the Medical Examiner's office in Schenectady County.

Sir Albert Schweitzer said, "Altruism is an essential component of those actions which lead to true happiness." Dr. Oram is a living example of this principle in his life. He cherished his work, his family and his friends rather than material possessions. He has given lectures, talks and seminars to numerous groups, including school children, physicians and senior citizens on varying subjects, including AIDS, Egyptian medicine, and parasitic infections, all on a voluntary basis. One of his missions in life was to help educate and improve the health of the public-at-large.

Dr. Oram was a content man, content with all of his heart. I believe it was God's gift to him. Random acts of kindness - doing good deeds without expecting anything in return - these are the hallmarks of a spiritually evolved individual such as Dr. Oram.

He was blessed with a loving wife, Joanne, who took wonderful care of him, and with lovely children. His countenance always uplifted our spirits, and everyone felt comfortable in his presence.

*　　*　　*

Daniel J. Rourke, MD

By Carolyn Jones-Assini, MD

Dr. Rourke, with his 6-foot-4-inch frame and booming bass voice, was an immense figure on the landscape of the Schenectady medical community. He was gentle and supportive, with a kind demeanor, though he was a force to be reckoned with if his patients' best interests were threatened. He was a master in communication and coordination of care with his consultants. He never wrote an order with out fully explaining it to the nurses, and never requested a consultation without speaking directly with the specialist.

He was born in Greenwich, NY in 1922. His father worked for the Delaware and Hudson Railroad and could ride the trains for free. Dan, a lifelong baseball fan, and his dad would often take the train to Albany to watch the Albany Senators. Years later, he was spotted at Heritage Park on a hot and humid Saturday afternoon, the only spectator dressed in a suit, tie and hat.

Dr. Rourke attended Notre Dame University and graduated from Georgetown University Medical School in 1947. He served a residency in Pathology at Wilson Memorial Hospital, in Johnson City, New York and a second residency in Internal Medicine at Ellis Hospital in 1949. He served as a Lieutenant in the US Navy Medical Corps on the USS Mount Olympus. After an honorable discharge he returned to finish his Internal Medicine residency. Dr. Rourke established his Internal Medicine practice on Union Street in 1953 and served Schenectady and surrounding communities until his retirement in 2005. His conscientiousness and integrity commanded respect and his colleagues recognized him as a natural leader. He was Chief of Staff at Ellis and served as Chairman of the Utilization Committee for many years. He was also an attending physician at Sunnyview and St Clare's.

Dan was an old-school physician. He answered his own telephone, always maintained Saturday office hours and only took one brief vacation in his 52 years of practice. When you called his office day or night, it was his deep voice that answered the phone. He practiced well into his eighties and, when it became more difficult for him to get around, he made his hospital rounds in a wheel chair. When asked about retirement, he answered, *"when you retire, you only have one thing to look forward to."* Dr. Rourke passed away in July 2009.

*   *   *

George D. Vlahides, MD

By Carolyn Jones-Assini, MD

Dr. George Vlahides never lost the joy of discovery when looking through his beloved microscope. Stepping into his office was stepping into bygone years, when the art and the science of medicine were melded together. With an enthusiastic wave of his hand, he would invite you to witness a wonder of his microscopic world. George prepared and examined his own LE preps a generation after ANA tests came into use. He was a beloved teacher for the Laboratory Technology school.

Dr. Vlahides was at his best at Friday morning Grand Rounds, during those years when almost the entire Department of Medicine (which included Dermatology, Neurology, General Practice, Emergency Medicine and Cardiology) attended. His questions and comments were educational for everyone in the room. He had a breadth and depth of clinical knowledge, drawn from his personal experiences and from the scientific literature. His consultation reports were usually three handwritten pages in length.

During the monthly administrative meetings, when discussion turned to a dispute between Ellis Hospital and Albany Medical Center, usually concerning referral patterns or the residency, George would explain that strained relations between Albany and Schenectady dated way back to the fur trade.

Dr. Vlahides was a congenial and compassionate man and made friends easily, especially at the YMCA, where he regularly exercised during the noon hour. His work ethic was legendary;

his office hours began at 7:00AM, much to the chagrin of his patients and staff, and he frequently worked until late in the evening.

Dr. Vlahides graduated from Erasmus Hall High School in Brooklyn, New York and from Columbia College in 1947 after serving in active duty during World War II from 1944-1946. With support from the GI bill, he attended New York Medical College, graduating in 1951. He began his medical practice in Schenectady in 1956, founded the Department of Special Hematology at Ellis and helped establish the Macdonald Oncology Hematology Unit in 1980.

George served as Chief of Medical Education at Ellis for many years. In this capacity, he supervised the freestanding residencies in Pathology, Obstetrics, Medicine and Surgery. He was the Division Chief of Hematology and, for several years in the mid-1970s, served as Acting Chief of Medicine. Dr. Vlahides was a physician who was determined to "die with his boots on." He practiced actively well into his seventies and, one evening, after working late at the hospital, he went home and suffered a stroke in his sleep. He never regained consciousness.

A Memorial Hematology Lecture series, established in his name, is a portion of his legacy as a physician, teacher, colleague and friend.

SECTION 3

**Medical Society
of the County of Schenectady, Inc.**

Recent Past Presidents

**June 2010
Membership and Elected Officers**

RECENT PAST PRESIDENTS

Medical Society of the County of Schenectady, Inc

Compiled by James M. Strosberg, MD

Year	President	Year	President
1960	Maurice Donovan, MD	1985	John Spring, MD
1961	Donald Walker, MD	1986	John Fulco, MD
1962	Joseph Cortesi, MD	1987	Kirk Panneton, MD
1963	Norman Kathan, MD	1988	Carl Paulsen, MD
1964	Morris Shapiro, MD	1989	Thomas Oram, MD
1965	Joseph Naumoff, MD	1990	Donald Wexler, MD
1966	Philip Parillo, MD	1991	William Busino, Jr., MD
1967	Raymond Byron, MD	1992	John Kennedy, Jr., MD
1968	Michael Tytko, MD	1993	Richard Brooks, MD
1969	Gerald Parkhurst, MD	1994	Peter Rienzi, MD
1970	Herbert Wright, Jr., MD	1995	James Strosberg, MD
1971	Gerald Haines, MD	1996	Robert Kennedy, MD
1972	John Clowe, MD	1997	Peter Purcell, MD
1973	Thomas McGarry, MD	1998	Lawrence Routenberg, MD
1974	John Kennedy, Sr., MD	1999	Nadarajah Balasubramaniam, MD
1975	Stewart Wagoner, MD	2000	Paul Skudder, MD
1976	Franklyn Hayford, MD	2001	John Angerosa, MD
1977	Robert Cassidy, MD	2002	William Anyaegbunam, MD
1978	Richard Lange, MD	2003	Carolyn Jones-Assini, MD
1979	Marvin Humphrey, MD	2004	Stewart Silvers, MD
1980	Robert Sullivan, MD	2005	Fouad Sattar, MD
1981	James Holmblad, MD	2006	Michael Jakubowski, MD
1982	Richard Gullott, MD	2007	John Assini, MD
1983	Marion Farlin, MD	2008	Louis Snitkoff, MD
1984	Charles Stamm, MD	2009	Bruce Barach, MD

Officers who served multiple terms without serving as President include Secretaries: William Farrell, MD, 1967-1975; Robert Sandroni, MD, 1976-1978; George Kehoe, MD, 1979-1983; Gary Wood, MD, 1996-1999; Gary Kronick, MD, 2001-2003; and Ali Mirza, MD, 2008-2009; Treasurers: Kurt Meyerhoff, MD, 1959-1962; Louis Tischler, MD, 1963-1966; Alexander Arony, MD, 1967-1973; Janis Best, MD, 1974-1984; Areta Pidwerbetsky, MD, 1996-2000.

Mark G. Adsit, M.D.
Specialty – Gastroenterology
Joined – May 7, 2003
New York Medical College 1983

Neema R. Afejuku-Adelaja, M.D.
Specialty – Family Practice
Joined – June 5, 2008
Medical School – University of Benin,
 Nigeria 1995

William I. Anyaegbunam, M.D.
Specialty – Obstetrics and Gynecology
Joined – February 4, 1997
Medical School – Royal College of Sau,
 Ireland

David C. Armenia, M.D.
Specialty – Cardiology
Joined – April 3, 1990
Medical School – St. Louis University 1983

Eric R. Aronowitz, M.D.
Specialty – Orthopedics
Joined – June 3, 2004
Medical School – SUNY 1994

John F. Assini, M.D.
Specialty – Rheumatology
Joined – June 7, 1979
Albany Medical College 1973

Afolake Awoyale, M.D.
Specialty – Family Medicine
Joined – NA
Medical School – Spartan University, SOM
 2005

Avinash Bachwani, M.D.
Specialty – Family Practice
Joined – December 1, 2005
Medical School – Rural Medical College,
 Loni, India

Ephraim E. Back, M.D.
Specialty – Family Practice
Joined – February 2, 1999
Medical School – SUNY Buffalo 1984

Arulnayagi Balasubramaniam
Specialty – Pathology
Joined – April 1, 1986
Medical School – June 1967

Nadarajah Balasubramaniam
Specialty – Pathology
Joined – December 3, 1981
Medical School – University of Ceylon 1967

Bruce K. Barach, M.D.
Specialty – Plastic Surgery
Joined – March 7, 1989
Medical School – SUNY Syracuse 1982

Donald A. Bentrovato, M.D.
Specialty – Urology
Joined – October 3, 1978
Medical School – St. Louis University 1973

Jessica D. Berman, M.D.
Specialty – Family Practice
Joined – December 5, 2008
Medical School – Boston University 2001

Karen Bleser, M.D.
Specialty: Internal Medicine
Joined Society – 4/6/10
Medical School – SUNY Syracuse 2000

James M. Boler, M.D.
Specialty – Orthopedics
Joined – April 10, 2007
Medical School – University of Maryland
    1995

George Boyar, M.D.
Specialty – Internal Medicine
Joined – May 4, 1993
Medical School – University of Guadalajara
    1981

Nelson M. Braslow, M.D.
Specialty – Internal Medicine and
    Pulmonary Medicine
Medical School – Harvard Medical School
    1975

Paul A. Brisson, M.D.
Specialty – Surgery
Joined – February 7, 1989
Medical School – St. George's University
    1982

Kemp W. Bundy, M.D.
Specialty – Allergy, Asthma and Immunology
Joined – December 3, 1009
Albany Medical College 2003

Michael Burke, M.D.
Specialty – Radiology
Joined – June 3, 1993
Albany Medical College 1982

William A. Busino, Jr., M.D.
Specialty – Internal Medicine
Joined – November 6, 1979
Albany Medical College 1975

Gilles Chapados, M.D.
Specialty – Otolaryngology
Joined – March 1986
Medical School – 1978

Lucie Capek, M.D.
Specialty – Plastic Surgery
Joined – December 3, 1996
Medical School – McGill University 1986

Cindy H. Chan, M.D.
Specialty – Internal Medicine
Joined – June 5, 2003
Medical School – McGill University 1995

Hee-Joo Cheon, M.D.
Specialty – Obstetrics and Gynecology
Joined – NA
NY Medical College 1992

Elaine Cheon-Lee, M.D.
Specialty – Obstetrics and Gynecology
Joined – December 4, 1997
Cornell University Medical School 1989

Siren R. Chudgar, M.D.
Specialty – Family Medicine
Joined – NA
Medical School – SUNY Syracuse 2000

Terence J. Clarke, M.D.
Specialty – General and Bariatric Surgery
Joined – NA
Medical School – Ross University 1997

David P. Cohen, M.D.
Specialty – Gastroenterology
Joined – December 3, 1993
Medical School – SUNY Brooklyn 1988

Kenneth A. Coleman, M.D.
Specialty – Cardiology
Joined – October 5, 2004
Medical School – SUNY Stony Brook 1999

John A. Collins, M.D.
Specialty – Otolaryngology
Joined – October 5, 1976
Medical School – University of Michigan

Alan T. Conlon, M.D.
Specialty – Family Practice
Joined – June 6, 2002
Medical School – SUNY Syracuse 1979

Glen Robert Cooley, M.D.
Specialty – Orthopedics
Joined – January 3, 1978
Medical School – University of Chicago
  1973

Ligaya P. Cosico, M.D.
Specialty – Pediatrics
Joined – November 5, 1974
Medical School – Far Eastern University
  1967

Peter Cospito, D.O.
Specialty – Interventional Cardiology
Joined – May 2, 1995
Chicago College of Osteopathic Medicine
  1984

Robert A. Crafts, M.D.
Specialty – Anesthesiology
Joined – October 7, 1975
University of Michigan School of Medicine

Dennis R. David, M.D.
Specialty – Surgery
Joined – March 1, 2005
Medical School – University of Santo Tomas
  1965

John F. DeFrancisco, M.D.
Specialty – Gastroenterology
Joined – May 3, 2005
Medical School - UNY 1998

Harry DePan, M.D.
Specialty – Cardiothoracic Surgery
Joined – 1991
Albany Medical College 1978

Michael A. DePetrillo, Jr., M.D.
Specialty – Anesthesiology
Joined – October 2, 1979
Columbia University, College of Physicians
& Surgeons 1975

Matthew R. DiCaprio, M.D.
Specialty – Orthopedic Surgery
Joined – NA
Medical School – SUNY Syracuse 1998

Y. Mesut Dincer, M.D.
Specialty – Internal Medicine
Joined – February 4, 1997
Medical. School Istanbul, Turkey 1983

John T. Dinius, M.D.
Specialty – Anesthesiology
Joined – June 3, 2004
Medical School – Indiana University School
of Medicine 1994

Robert J. Donohue, Jr., M.D.
Specialty – Internal Medicine
Joined – October 6, 1998
Medical School – SUNY Syracuse 1993

Zofia W. Drzymakski, M.D.
Specialty – Family Practice
Joined – June 6, 2002
Medical Academy, Gdansk, Poland 1984

W.J. Duke Dufresne, M.D.
Specialty – Family Practice
Joined – December 5, 1989
Tufts University School of Medicine 1981

Gary R. Dunkerley, M.D.
Specialty – Family Practice
Joined – January 5, 1982
Hahnemann Medical College 1975

Paul Dworkin, M.D.
Specialty – Cardiology
Joined – November 2, 1982
Columbia University College of Physicians &
Surgeons 1977

Carolyn Eaton, M.D.
Specialty – Family Practice
Joined – June 6, 2002
Medical School – SUNY Syracuse

Lawrence B. Eisenberg, M.D
Specialty – Anesthesiology
Joined – October 7, 1975
Albany Medical College

Clifford M. Elson, M.D.
Specialty – Obstetrics and Gynecology
Joined – December 8, 1977
Medical School – New York University 1973

Eric Engelmyer, M.D.
Specialty – Urology
Joined – May 4, 1999
Hahnemann Medical College 1990

Carl Englebardt, M.D.
Specialty – Plastic Surgery
Joined – November 2, 1982
Medical School – University of Chicago
1972

Martin S. Farber, M.D.
Specialty – Internal Medicine
Joined – November 6, 1984
Albert Einstein College of Medicine 1979

Angel Fermin, M.D.
Specialty – Radiologist
Joined – October 5, 1993
Medical School – Autonoma Santo Domingo
    1981

Leonides T. Fernando, M.D.
Specialty – Radiology
Joined – April 7, 1992
Medical School – University of Santo Tomas
    1972

Bradley A. Ford, M.D.
Specialty – Pediatrics
Joined – June 6, 2002
Albany Medical College 1978

David L. Ford, M.D.
Specialty – Surgery
Joined – October 2, 2009
Howard University Medical School 1993

Patricia A. Fox, M.D.
Specialty – Plastic & Reconstructive Surgery
Joined – April 1, 1980
Medical School – SUNY Brooklyn 1972

Melissa M. Foye-Petrillo, D.O.
Specialty – Pediatrics
Joined – February 7, 2007
NY College of Osteopathic Medicine 2002

Lynn Fraterrigo-Boler, M.D.
Specialty – Ophthalmology
Joined – February 6, 2007
Medical School - SUNY Syracuse 2005

John D. Fulco, M.D.
Specialty – Radiology
Joined – October 2, 1979
Medical School – University of Bologna
    1974

Joseph P. Fusella, D.O.
Specialty – Family Practice
Joined – December 1992
NY College of Osteopathic Medicine 1987

Frank L. Genovese, M.D.
Specialty – Neurosurgery
Joined – December 5, 1991
Chicago Medical School 1985

Joseph Gerardi, M.D.
Specialty – Obstetrics and Gynecology
Joined – December 3, 1992
Albany Medical College 1979

Robert E. Gerstenbluth, M.D.
Specialty – Urology
Joined – May 3, 2005
Medical School – SUNY Buffalo 1998

George J. Giokas, M.D.
Specialty – Internal Medicine
Joined – January 3, 1984
Medical School – George Washington
    University 1980

Steven M. Goldberg, M.D.
Specialty – Internal Medicine
Joined – December 1990
Medical School – SUNY Brooklyn 1983

Michael S. Goldstoff, M.D.
Specialty – Anesthesiology
Joined – February 7, 1995
Columbia University College of Physicians
    and Surgeons1987

Brian M. Gordon, M.D.
Specialty – Orthopedic Surgery
Joined – October 3, 2000
Medical School – SUNY Syracuse 1993

Anthony N. Gregory, M.D.
Specialty – Dermatology
Joined – December 6, 2007
Medical School – University of North
    Carolina, Chapel Hill 1984

Michael P. Grossman, M.D.
Specialty – Obstetrics and Gynecology
Joined – May 2009
Michigan State University College of
    Human Medicine 1997

Eugene C. Haber, M.D.
Specialty – Family Practice
Joined – June 6, 2002
Medical School – Ross University, Dominica
    1985

Joseph L. Hayes, D.O.
Specialty – Internal Medicine
Joined – NA
NY College of Osteopathic Medicine

Marc E. Heller, M.D.
Specialty – Anesthesia
Joined – April 2004
Medical School – SUNY Buffalo1973

Paul Hendrickson, D.O.
Specialty – Anesthesiology
Joined – December 1, 1994
Philadelphia College of Osteopathic
    Medicine 1990

Lynn Hickey, M.D.
Specialty – Pediatrics/Internal Medicine
Joined – February 6, 2007
Albany Medical College 1999

Louis C. Ianniello, M.D.
Specialty – Family Practice
Joined – June 6, 2002
Medical School - St. George's University
    1989

Malene K. Ingram, M.D.
Specialty - General Surgery
Joined – May 1, 2007
Michigan State University – College of
    Human Medicine

Michael S. Jakubowski, M.D.
Specialty – Anesthesiology
Joined – November 2, 1976
Tufts University School of Medicine

Gerardus Lee Jameson, M.D.
Specialty – Gastroenterology
Joined – December 1995
Albany Medical College 1989

Steven R. Jarrett, M.D.
Specialty – Physical Medicine and
    Rehabilitation
Joined – December 1, 1983
Chicago Medical School 1969

John W. Jaski, M.D.
Specialty – Medical Oncology
Joined – October 5, 1976
Cornell University Medical College

Piotr Jaworowski, M.D.
Specialty - Family Practice
Joined Society – 4/6/10
Medical School – Medical University Gdansk
    1997

Carolyn Jones-Assini, M.D.
Specialty – Internal Medicine
Joined – June 1, 1995
Medical School – University of Iowa, 1973

Ron T. Kassof, M.D.
Specialty – Anesthesiology
Joined – May 1992
Albany Medical College 1987

Sanjiv Kayastha, M.D.
Specialty – Plastic Surgery
Joined – May 2, 2006
Medical School – SUNY Buffalo 1999

Jonathan Kemp, M.D.
Specialty – Anesthesiology
Joined – December 1995
Medical School – NY Medical College 1990

John J. Kennedy, Jr., M.D.
Specialty – Ophthalmology
Joined – January 6, 1981
Medical School – University of Guadalajara
    1975

Robert J. Kennedy, M.D.
Specialty – Ophthalmology
Joined – February 6, 1985
Medical School – Georgetown University
    1979

David D. Kim, M.D.
Specialty – Anesthesiology
Joined – December 1992
Medical School – Temple University 1987

Jay A. Kravitz, M.D.
Specialty – Family Medicine
Joined – May 7, 2002
Medical School – St. Georges University
    1982

Denise A. Lawrence, M.D.
Specialty – Family Practice
Joined – June 6, 2002
Medical School – SUNY Syracuse

Arthur Lee, M.D.
Specialty – Family Practice
Joined – June 6, 2002
Albany Medical College 1990

Ernest Jay Lee, M.D.
Specialty – Otolaryngology
Joined – December 3, 1998
Medical School – University of Rochester
    1990

Robert G. Leupold, M.D.
Specialty – Orthopedics
Joined – November 30 1979
Medical School – SUNY Brooklyn 1967

David M. Liebers, M.D.
Specialty – Infectious Diseases
Joined – November 1, 1988
Medical School – University of Rochester
    1982

Dean J. Limeri, M.D.
Specialty – Internal Medicine/Pediatrics
Joined – December 1990
Albany Medical College 1983

Barry S. Lindenberg, M.D.
Specialty – Cardiology
Joined – December 1, 1983
Albany Medical College

Harry D. Lindman, Jr., D.O.
Specialty – Family Practice
Joined – June 6, 2002
Philadelphia College of Osteopathic
    Medicine 1992

James Litynski, M.D.
Specialty – Gastroenterology
Joined – December 7, 1995
Albany Medical College 1985

Melvyn A. Lobo, M.D.
Specialty – Family Practice
Joined – February 6, 2007
Dow Medical College 1984

Douglas A. Long, M.D.
Specialty – Cardiology
Joined – March 6, 1990
Medical School – UMD New Jersey 1982

Franklin B. Longo, M.D.
Specialty – Ophthalmology
Joined – May 1991
Medical College of Wisconsin 1983

Teresa E. McCarthy, M.D.
Specialty – OB/GYN
Joined – January 8, 1974
University of Philippines College of
    Medicine 1966

Brian A. McDonald, M.D.
Specialty – Pulmonary and Critical Care
    Medicine
Joined – February 4, 2008
Columbia University College of Physicians
    and Surgeons 1997

Gerard J. McGrinder, M.D.
Specialty – Obstetrics and Gynecology
Joined – December 1993
Medical School – University of Guadalajara
    1987

Robert McKay, M.D.
Specialty – Surgery
Joined – February 6, 2007
Medical School – Memorial University of
    Newfoundland 1984

Howard S. Malamood, M.D.
Specialty – Gastroenterology
Joined – May 2005
Albany Medical College 1981

Denis P. Manor, M.D.
Specialty – Cardiology
Joined – June 1, 1989
Medical School – SUNY Syracuse 1982

Renata N. Mazzei-Klokiw, M.D.
Specialty: Family Practice
Joined Society – 4/6/10
Medical School – University of Santo Tomas
1998

Philip J. Mika, M.D.
Specialty – Internal Medicine
Joined – February 1, 1977
Ohio State University College of Medicine
1972

Ali Mirza, M.D.
Specialty – Internal Medicine
Joined – February 6, 2001
Medical School – University of Cairo

Zoser Mohamed, M.D.
Specialty – Psychiatry
Joined – May 2, 1995
Medical School – University of Cairo 1977

Fe A. Mondragon, M.D.
Specialty – Obstetrics and Gynecology
Joined – July 9, 1981
Medical School – University of Santo Tomas
1969

Donald R. Morere, Jr., M.D.
Specialty – Gastroenterology
Joined – May 2, 1982
Albany Medical College 1982

Eric D. Moses, M.D.
Specialty – Anesthesiology
Joined – NA
Medical School – American University of the
Caribbean 2003

Christine M. Murphy, M.D.
Specialty – Internal Medicine
Joined – June 6, 2002
Medical School – University of Maryland
1985

Kevin Murphy, M.D.
Specialty – Anesthesiology
Joined – February 2, 1988
Medical School – University of Iowa 1983

Brian Navarro, M.D.
Specialty – Family Practice
Joined – June 5, 2003
Albany Medical College 1999

Andalib Nawab, M.D.
Specialty – Internal Medicine
Joined – NA
Aga Khan Karachi Medical College 1993

Lynn T. Nicolson, M.D.
Specialty – Physical Medicine and
Rehabilitation
Joined – March 7, 1989
Albany Medical College 1983

John A. Nolan, M.D.
Specialty – Cardiology
Joined – December 1, 1983
Albany Medical College 1977

Michael P. Novak, M.D.
Specialty – Internal Medicine and
    Nephrology
Joined – October 3, 1968
Albert Einstein College of Medicine 1962

Arthur H. Ostrov, M.D.
Specialty – Gastroenterology
Joined – October 20, 1978
Medical School – University of Bologna
    1975

Phillip D. Pan, M.D.
Specialty – Neonatology
Joined – April 10, 2007
Brown Medical School 1998

Vishnudas P. Panemanglore, MBBS
Specialty – Bariatric Surgery
Joined – October 2, 2007
Kasturba Medical School 1992

Kirk R. Panneton, M.D.
Specialty – Internal Medicine
Joined – December 10, 1980
Medical School – Boston University 1977

Robert J. Parkes, M.D.
Specialty – Cardiology
Joined – February 4, 1986
Medical School – SUNY Buffalo 1980

Pratima S. Patel, M.D.
Specialty – Pediatrics
Joined – May 6, 1975
Baroda Medical College 1964

Shailesh R. Patel, M.D.
Specialty – Internal Medicine
Joined – December 6, 1997
Medical School –Baroda Medical College
    1982

Joseph Pazienza, M.D.
Specialty – Radiology
Joined – October 4, 1994
Albany Medical College 1987

Elyse Pearson, M.D.
Specialty – Anesthesiology
Joined – NA
Medical School – SUNY Brooklyn1984

Charles Craig Peterson, M.D.
Specialty – Cardiology
Joined – June 5, 1997
Tufts University School of Medicine 1986

John M. Petrillo, D.O.
Specialty – Family Practice
Joined – NA
New York College of Osteopathic Medicine
    2003

Chittaranjan Prasad, M.D.
Specialty – Internal Medicine and Pediatrics
Joined – October 2, 2007
Medical School – Rajendra Medical College
    1980

Darin M. Price, D.O.
Specialty – Pediatrics
Joined – June 6, 2002
New York College of Osteopathic Medicine
 1996

Peter F. Purcell, M.D.
Specialty – Gastroenterology
Joined – November 6, 1979
Cornell University College of Medicine 1974

Shaheen B. Rahman, M.D.
Specialty – Urology
Joined – December 4, 1997
Albany Medical College 1992

Raphy Rebanal, M.D.
Specialty – Surgery
Joined – January 8, 1980
Medical School – University of Santo Tomas

Herbert Reich, M.D.
Specialty – Cardiothoracic Surgery
Joined – October 15, 1997
Medical School – SUNY Stony Brook 1988

John C. Richards, M.D.
Specialty – Orthopedics
Joined – October 1, 1974
McGill University Medical College 1965

Peter Rienzi, M.D.
Specialty – Internal Medicine
Joined – November 1, 1988
New York University School of Medicine
 1982

David R. Rockwell, M.D.
Specialty – Infectious Diseases
Joined – December 7, 1978
Medical School – St. Louis University 1973

Lawrence J. Routenberg, M.D.
Specialty – Anesthesiology
Joined – October 2, 1979
Medical College of Wisconsin 1975

Peter J. Runge, M.D.
Specialty – Cardiology
Joined – November 2, 1971
Medical School – George Washington
 University 1965

Bradford Ruthberg, M.D.
Specialty – Radiology
Joined – February 1988
Medical School – University of Miami 1980

Judith C. Ruthberg, M.D.
Specialty – Diagnostic Radiology
Joined – December 6, 2007
Medical School – University of Miami 1980

Huseyin Sahin, M.D.
Specialty – Surgery
Joined – April 3, 2001
Medical School – University of Hacettepe
 Medical School 1972

James Saperstone, M.D.
Specialty – Pediatrics
Joined – June 6, 2002
Medical School – University of Virginia
 1978

Fouad Sattar, M.D.
Specialty – Obstetrics and Gynecology
Joined – December 7, 1995
Medical School – University of Cairo 1963

Victor A. Schingo, Jr., M.D.
Specialty – Plastic Surgery
Joined – May 1, 2001
New York Medical College 1992

Howard R. Schlossberg, M.D.
Specialty – Hematology and Oncology
Joined – April 10, 2007
Medical School – Temple University 1999

Marvin Schwartz, M.D.
Specialty – Radiology
Joined – NA
New York Medical College 1991

Steven Seminer, M.D.
Specialty – Anesthesiology
Joined – December 1990
Albany Medical College 1985

Edward M. Sessa, M.D.
Specialty – Pediatrics
Joined – June 12, 1979
Cornell University Medical School 1973

Kenneth Shapiro, M.D.
Specialty – Physical Medicine and
    Rehabilitation
Joined – March 1991
Mount Sinai Medical School 1985

George T. Shelton, M.D.
Specialty – Physical Medicine and
    Rehabilitation
Joined – 1989
Albany Medical College 1976

Sonya M. Sidhu, M.D.
Specialty – Family Practice
Joined – 2005
Medical University of Lublin 2001

Stewart A. Silvers, M.D.
Specialty – Hematology/Oncology
Joined – November 1, 1977
Medical School – University of Pittsburgh
    1972

Richard Simmons, M.D.
Specialty – Neurology
Joined – June 3, 2010
Drexel University College of Medicine 2003

Mitchell S. Singer, M.D.
Specialty – Dermatology
Joined – April 1986
Albany Medical College 1981

Harbans Singh, M.D.
Specialty – Pathology
Joined – 1986
Amritsar Medical College 1960

Catherine M. Smitas, M.D.
Specialty – Internal Medicine
Joined – 2008
University of Rochester School of Medicine
    2002

William James Smith, M.D.
Specialty – Orthopedics
Joined – December 6, 1990
Boston University School of Medicine 1984

Louis S. Snitkoff, M.D.
Specialty – Internal Medicine
Joined – June 5, 1980
Medical School – SUNY Brooklyn 1977

Vincent M. Somaio, M.D.
Specialty – Physical Medicine and
    Rehabilitation
Joined – February 7, 2006
Albany Medical College

Juho Song, M.D.
Specialty – Radiology
Joined – December 6, 2001
Medical School – Seoul National University
    1981

Michael Sonnekalb, M.D.
Specialty – Pediatrics
Joined – June 6, 2002
Albany Medical College 1981

Karen Spinelli, M.D.
Specialty – Pediatrics
Joined – December 1995
Robert Wood Johnson School of Medicine
    1985

Sheldon B. Staunton, M.D.
Specialty – Neurology
Joined – November 3, 1970
Albany Medical College 1964

Arthur Stevens, M.D.
Specialty – Internal Medicine
Joined – March 1991
Albany Medical College 1984

Peter H. Stier, M.D.
Specialty – Obstetrics and Gynecology
Joined – NA
Medical School – Robert Wood Johnson
    School of Medicine 1995

Strosberg, James M., M.D.
Specialty – Rheumatology
Joined – November 2, 1976
Medical School – SUNY Buffalo 1967

Iftikhar A. Syed, M.D.
Specialty – Surgery
Joined – July 1, 1980
Medical School – Liaouat Medical College
    1972

Sandra Taccad-Reyes, M.D.
Specialty – Endocrinology
Joined – June 5, 2003
Medical School – University of the East 1988

Muhammad S. Tai, M.D.
Specialty – Hematology and Oncology
Joined – June 5, 2003
Medical School – Dow Medical College 1985

Alexander Tenenboym, M.D.
Specialty – Anesthesiology
Joined – NA
Medical School – Rush Medical College
    1988

William R. Tetreault, M.D.
Specialty – Family Practice
Joined – June 6, 2002
Albany Medical College 1986

Richard B. Toll, M.D.
Specialty – Internal Medicine
Joined – June 7, 1979
Albany Medical College 1976

Benoit A. Tonneau, M.D.
Specialty – Internal Medicine
Joined – October 3, 2000
Medical School – Catholic University of
    Louvain 1988

Beatrice H. Tsao, M.D.
Specialty – Obstetrics and Gynecology
Joined – May 4, 1999
Harvard Medical School 1988

William M. Vacca, M.D.
Specialty – Cardiology
Joined – November 4, 1980
Creighton University School of Medicine
    1974

Francois M. Vachon, D.O.
Specialty – Family Practice
Joined – June 6, 2002
Medical School – New England College of
    Osteopathic Medicine 1983

Arthur R. Vakiener, M.D.
Specialty – Cardiology
Joined – February 7, 1995
Albany Medical College 1979

Elizabeth A. Valentine, M.D.
Specialty – Hematology and Oncology
Joined – December 1992
Medical School – SUNY Syracuse 1983

George Vassolas, M.D.
Specialty – Cardiology
Joined – 1995
Albany Medical College 1986

Theresa Viola, M.D.
Specialty – Family Practice
Joined – June 6, 2002
Albany Medical College 1989

Venkateswararao Voleti, M.D.
Specialty – Internal Medicine and
    Nephrology
Joined – February 4, 1992
Kurnool Medical College 1978

Eric M. Wagle, M.D.
Specialty – Radiology
Joined – October 7, 1987
Medical School – University of Maryland

Laurence A. Weiner, M.D.
Specialty – Internal Medicine
Joined – November 4, 1975
University of Illinois Medical School

Steven H. Weitz, M.D.
Specialty –Cardiology
Joined – April 9, 2002
New York University School of Medicine
    1992

Zeev Weitz, M.D.
Specialty –Internal Medicine
Joined – April 2, 1996
Medical School – Technion 1983

Gary A. Williams, M.D.
Specialty – Orthopedics
Joined – December 7, 1978
Medical School – University of Pennsylvania
   1970

Gary Wood, M.D.
Specialty – Radiology
Joined – November 3, 1987
Medical School – SUNY Syracuse 1977

Margaret Woods, M.D.
Specialty – Pediatrics
Joined – June 6, 1996
New York University School of Medicine
   1991

Norbert J. Woods, M.D.
Specialty – Pediatrics
Joined – January 3, 1978
New York Univ. School of Medicine 1974

Nasrene R. Yadegari-Lewis, M.D.
Specialty – Internal Medicine and Pediatrics
Joined – April 10, 2007
University of Rochester School of Medicine
   1999

Richard Yan, M.D.
Specialty – Pediatrics
Joined – June 6, 2002
Medical School – University of the East 1973

LIFE MEMBERS

Richard W. Akin, M.D.
Specialty – Anesthesiology
Joined – January 8, 1985
University of California School of Medicine
    1959

Patrick M. Albano, M.D.
Specialty – Orthopedic Surgery
Joined – November 2, 1971
Medical School – Loyola University 1961

Joseph R. Asaro, M.D.
Specialty – Radiology
Joined – October 5, 1976
University of Palermo, School of Medicine

James B. Bell, M.D.
Specialty – Anesthesiology
Joined – November 6, 1956
Medical School – Glasgow University 1947

Janis L. Best, M.D.
Specialty – Psychiatry
Joined – October 5, 1954
Albany Medical College 1949

Bernard R. Blais, M.D.
Specialty – Ophthalmology
Joined – March 6, 1990
Medical School – University of Vermont
    1958

Robert M. Blumenberg, M.D.
Specialty – Vascular Surgery
Joined – November 5, 1968
Albany Medical College 1959

Miguel A. Cabral, M.D.
Specialty – Cardiology
Joined – November 2, 1971
Medical School – Cordoba University 1960

Louise H. Chase, M.D.
Specialty – Pathology
Joined – December 5, 1968
Albany Medical College 1947

Hong Kyu Cheon, M.D.
Specialty – Obstetrics and Gynecology
Joined – April 4, 1972
Medical School – Catholic Medical College,
    Seoul 1966

Janet B. Christman, M.D.
Specialty – Pathology
Joined – April 6, 1971
Medical School – Case Western Reserve
    1958

Dominic R. Cirincione, M.D.
Specialty – Gastroenterology
Joined – October 3, 1950
Loyola University School of Medicine 1948

John L. Clowe, M.D.
Specialty – General Practice
Joined – October 4, 1949
Albany Medical College 1946

Leonard F. Combi, M.D.
Specialty – Pediatrics
Joined – March 4, 1969
Medical School – University of Bologna
    1962

James K. Cooley, M.D.
Specialty – Family Practice
Joined – February 6, 1996
Loma Linda Medical School1958

Dennis F. Corbett, M.D.
Specialty – Ophthalmology
Joined – NA
Seton Hall College of Medicine 1963

James F. Cunningham, M.D.
Specialty – Psychiatry
Joined – January 31, 1964
Medical School – Howard University 1945

Carlos de la Rocha, M.D.
Specialty – Surgery
Joined – June 2, 1966
Santo Domingo Medical School 1958

Angela Diamond, M.D.
Specialty – Obstetrics and Gynecology
Joined – May 27, 1955
Medical School – SUNY Syracuse

Martha S. DiOrio, M.D.
Specialty – General Practice
Joined – February 7, 1950
University of Maryland Medical School
    1943

John A. Dolan, M.D.
Specialty – Orthopedics
Joined – March 25, 1970
Medical School – George Washington
    University 1961

Roland Doucet, M.D.
Specialty – Obstetrics and Gynecology
Joined – November 1, 1966
Medical School – Queen's University 1962

Eugene E. Drago, M.D.
Specialty – Cardiology
Joined – October 1, 1957
Medical School – Georgetown University
    1955

Marion J. Farlin, M.D.
Specialty – Internal Medicine and
    Endocrinology
Joined – November 2, 1965
Women's Medical College of Pennsylvania
    1959

Edmond J. Fitzgibbon, M.D.
Specialty – Surgery
Joined – October 4, 1955
Long Island College of Medicine 1947

Julius Gelber, M.D.
Specialty – Urology
Joined – December 7, 1950
Medical School – University of Maryland
    1941

Michael L. Gelfand, M.D.
Specialty – General & Vascular Surgery
Joined – November 7, 1972
Columbia University College of Physicians
    and Surgeons 1964

Constance L. Glasgow, M.D.
Specialty – Pediatrics
Joined – February 1, 1966
Medical School – SUNY Brooklyn 1960

John M. Gold, M.D.
Specialty – Urology
Joined – October 7, 1975
Medical School – SUNY Buffalo

Steven J. Goodman, M.D.
Specialty – Plastic Surgery
Joined – February 3, 1981
Albany Medical College 1975

John J. Gorman, M.D.
Specialty – Radiology
Joined – December 2, 1965
Medical School – SUNY Syracuse 1958

Anthony F. Guidarelli, M.D.
Specialty – Orthopedics
Joined – November 5, 1974
Medical School – University of Bologna
    1966

Richard F. Gullott, M.D.
Specialty – Pulmonary Medicine
Joined – December 7, 1967
Medical School – UMD New Jersey 1962

Lilia S. Guzman, M.D.
Specialty – Internal Medicine
Joined – January 6, 1981
Medical School – University of Santo Tomas
    1955

Gerald L. Haines, M.D.
Specialty – Neurosurgery
Joined – April 7, 1953
University of Vermont Medical School 1944

Jesse T. Henderson, M.D.
Specialty – General Practice
Joined – October 6, 1959
Howard University School of Medicine 1954

K. Khossrow Heravi, M.D.
Specialty – Pathology
Joined – November 3, 1987
Tehran Medical University 1967

James E. Holmblad, M.D.
Specialty – Orthopedics
Joined – January 6, 1953
University of Pennsylvania Medical School
    1946

Seymour A. Horwitz, M.D.
Specialty – Internal Medicine
Joined – July 10, 1948
Albany Medical College 1939

Gerardus S. Jameson, M.D.
Specialty – Endocrinology
Joined – October 1, 1963
Albany Medical College 1959

William J. Jameson, Jr., M.D.
Specialty – Obstetrics and Gynecology
Joined – December 1, 1955
New York Medical College 1951

Frank W. Jones, M.D.
Specialty – Internal Medicine
Joined – January 26, 1954
Albany Medical College 1946

Grace G. Jorgensen, M.D.
Specialty – Obstetrics and Gynecology
Joined – October 4, 1955
New York Medical College 1954

Bernard McEvoy, M.D.
Specialty – Dermatology
Joined – January 1970
Albany Medical College 1961

James R. Kennedy, M.D.
Specialty – Pediatrics
Joined – December 6, 1962
Albany Medical College 1957

Akula V. Krishna, M.D.
Specialty – Surgery
Joined – December 2, 1976
Medical School – Osmania Medical College

Richard H. Lange M.D.
Specialty – Internal Medicine and Nuclear
 Medicine
Joined – October 6, 1953
New York Medical College 1948

Oscar Lirio, M.D.
Specialty – Surgery
Joined – March 3, 1970
University of Santo Tomas 1960

Joseph Loffredo, M.D.
Specialty – Pediatrics
Joined – November 1, 1963
Albany Medical College 1958

Roger J. Malebranche, M.D.
Specialty – General & Vascular Surgery
Joined – November 3, 1970
Medical School – Faculte de Medecine, 1957

Lewis J. Marola, M.D.
Specialty – Obstetrics and Gynecology
Joined – November 2, 1965
Medical School – University of Bologna
 1960

Frank G. Marsh, M.D.
Specialty – Internal Medicine
Joined – December 1964
Albany Medical College

Gerald Matura, M.D.
Specialty – Cardiology
Joined – July 6, 1948
Long Island College of Medicine

Bernard McEvoy, M.D.
Specialty – Dermatology
Joined – January 29, 1970
Albany Medical College 1961

Dominick Mele, M.D.
Specialty – Pediatric
Joined – May 4, 1948
Albany Medical College 1941

Robert A. Mitchell, M.D.
Specialty – Psychiatry
Joined – March 19, 2001
Medical School – University of Aberdeen
    1950

Donald R. Morton, M.D.
Specialty – Radiology
Joined – October 19, 1971
Medical School –University of Vermont
    1961

Aziz Nabi, M.D.
Specialty – Internal Medicine
Joined – November 1, 1966
Medical School – University of Brussels 1960

Navin S. Pardanani, M.D.
Specialty – Obstetrics and Gynecology
Joined – May 6, 1986
Medical School – Seth Medical College 1961

Carl A. Paulsen, M.D.
Specialty – Orthopedics
Joined – April 1, 1969
Albany Medical College 1958

Charles E. Peterson, M.D.
Specialty – Internal Medicine
Joined – November 5, 1963
Tulane University School of Medicine 1959

Robert J. Pletman, M.D.
Specialty – Urology
Joined – October 2, 1962
Medical School – SUNY Buffalo 1954

Alan I. Posner, M.D.
Specialty – Anesthesiology
Joined – December 28, 1967
Chicago Medical School 1960

Arnold B. Ritterband, M.D.
Specialty – Internal Medicine
Joined – October 6, 1959
Columbia University. College of Physicians
    and Surgeons 1950

Robert E. Sandroni, M.D.
Specialty – Internal Medicine
Joined – October 4, 1955
Long Island College of Medicine 1949

Pablo Schapiro, M.D.
Specialty – Pediatrics
Joined – October 3, 1968
Universidad de Chile Medical School 1961

Alvin D. Schwartz, M.D.
Specialty – Internal Medicine
Joined – December 3, 1964
New York University College of Medicine

Kanakaiahnavara R. Shankar, M.D.
Specialty – Cardiology
Joined – November 6, 1973
Medical School – University of Mysore 1953

Young J. Sim, M.D.
Specialty – Pathology
Joined – April 4, 1978
Medical School – EWHA University College
    of Medicine 1965

John M. Spring, M.D.
Specialty – Orthopedics
Joined – November 4, 1969
Medical School – Georgetown University
    1962

Charles F. Stamm, M.D.
Specialty – Radiology
Joined – October 4, 1960
Medical School – Temple University School
    of Medicine 1954

Robert H. Tafrate, M.D.
Specialty – Pulmonary Medicine
Joined – November 2, 1971
Medical School – University of Bologna
    1965

Clifford M. Tepper, M.D.
Specialty – Pediatrics
Joined – November 6, 1951
Columbia University College of Physicians
    and Surgeons 1946

Bruno P. Tolge, M.D.
Specialty – Neurology
Joined – October 3, 1968
Albany Medical College 1961

Jack L. Underwood, M.D.
Specialty – Psychology
Joined – November 6, 1962
Medical School – Howard University 1958

Elizabeth Veeder, M.D.
Specialty – Internal Medicine
Joined – June 1955
Albany Medical College 1946

Louis F. Wertalik, M.D.
Specialty – Hematology
Joined – November 6, 1973
Medical School – SUNY Buffalo 1967

Zdenek F. Zobal, M.D.
Specialty – General Practice
Joined – April 4, 1972
Medical School – Masaryk's University 1958

HONORARY MEMBERS

Robert A. Breault, M.D.
Specialty – Surgery
Joined – October 6, 1953
Albany Medical College 1947

Robert J. Cassidy. M.D.
Specialty – Neurology
Joined – November 3, 1959
Albany Medical College 1953

Raymond K. Kelly, M.D.
Specialty – Anesthesiology
Joined – June 2002
New York Medical College 1955

John T. Sheridan, M.D.
Specialty –Anesthesiology
Joined – October 2, 1956
New York Medical College 1953

COMMITTEES AND OFFICERS

Compiled by James M. Strosberg, MD

Like many other organizations, the Medical Society uses committees to help conduct its business. There were so many committees that members were often appointed to serve on several. Meeting schedules vary depending upon the role of the committee. These were the committees appointed in 1970:

Legislative, Public Relations, Program, Property, Public Health and Education, Alcoholism, Cancer, Diabetes Detection, Drug Abuse, Environmental Health, Hearing, Heart, Industrial Health, Ophthalmology, Aging, Advisory Committee to the Practical Nurses, Advisory Committee to the Department of Social Services, Committee on Standards of Practice for Doctors and Lawyers, Community Services, Comprehensive Health Planning Committee, Constitution and By-Laws, Entertainment, Health Education, Historian, Hospitals and Professional Relations, Insurance, Liaison with Clergy, Maternal Welfare and Perinatal Mortality, Mediation, Medical Economics, Medical Review, Photographic, Parliamentarian, Philanthropic Trust Fund, Pharmacy, Professional Liability Insurance and Advisory Committee, Red Cross Advisory Committee, Representatives to the Board of Directors of Blue Shield, Scholarship, Sick, and 7 miscellaneous delegates to various community and medical organizations including the Fourth District Branch of MSSNY. Not listed above were committees to the Boys Club, Girls Club and Carver Community Center. The Milk Committee and the Deadbeat Committee were disbanded by 1970. In addition, the list does not include the Nominating Committee, Compensation Committee, Delegates and Alternate Delegates to MSSNY, and the Board of Censors.

Over the years, the number of committees has decreased significantly. The 2009-2010 elected officers of the Society are:

President	Bruce Barach, MD
President-Elect	Jonathan Kemp, MD
Secretary	Ali Mirza, MD
Treasurer	Terence Clarke, MD
Board of Censors	Malene Ingram, MD
	Brian McDonald, MD
	Judith Ruthberg, MD
	Fouad Sattar, MD
	Sonya Sidhu-Izzo, MD
	Louis Snitkoff, MD
	Gary Wood, MD
Workers' Compensation Committee	Richard Gullott, MD
	Ali Mirza, MD (alternate)
Delegates to MSSNY	Carolyn Jones-Assini, MD
	John Kennedy, Jr., MD
	Lawrence Routenberg, MD
Alternates	John Angerosa, MD
	Lynn Fraterrigo-Boler, MD
	Sonya Sidhu-Izzo, MD
	Margaret Woods, MD
Nominating Committee	Richard D'Ascoli, MD
	Gerardus L. Jameson, MD
	Robert Kennedy, MD
	Phillip Pan, MD
	Fouad Sattar, MD
	Louis Snitkoff, MD